PRAISE FOR OTHER BOOKS BY JUDY ALLEN

EVENT PLANNING

The Ultimate Guide to Successful Meetings, Corporate Events, Fundraising Galas, Conferences, Conventions, Incentives and Other Events

(ISBN: 978-0-471-64412-5)

"Allen is a good teacher. Wise planners will add *Event Planning* to their personal reference library as a useful working guide."
—*Meeting Professional Magazine*

"A blueprint for executing events for 50 or 2,000, with budgets of a few thousand dollars to hundreds of thousands."
—*Success Magazine*

"*Event Planning* will save beginning event planners from plenty of heartbreak and headaches."
—*Lisa Hurley, Editor,* Special Events Magazine

"*Event Planning* gives readers a blueprint for planning and executing special events with flair. Consider the book as preventative maintenance."
—*Sales Promotion Magazine*

"A guide to well planned events. *Event Planning* is a must for any PR maven."
—*Marketing Magazine*

"This book will be a help to all event planners, from rank beginners to seasoned professionals. It provides excellent guidelines as well as helpful details."
—*Katherine Kossuth, Director of Operations and Special Events, Canadian Film Centre*

THE BUSINESS OF EVENT PLANNING

Behind-the-Scenes Secrets of Successful Special Events

(ISBN: 978-0-470-83188-5)

"*The Business of Event Planning* is a must-read for those in the event planning business. Strategic in thought and design and user-friendly in presentation, it literally tells you the paths to follow and the pitfalls to avoid. Well told, with examples to follow and stories to relate to, it's the 'how-to' that's a 'must-do' for the meetings, incentive, and event planning industry."
—*Peggy Whitman, President, Society of Incentive & Travel Executives; and Western Regional Sales Director, Marriott Incentive Awards*

"Written for anyone who has to prepare dynamite meetings and special events, *The Business of Event Planning* is your bible and a must-have desktop reference. Thanks, Judy Allen! You saved the day!"
—*Susan Fenner Ph.D., Manager, Education and Professional Development, International Association of Administrative Professionals (IAAP)*

"Guidance for new planners, reminders for experienced ones, and useful tips for everyone. This book has it all! It's the key that unlocks the mystery behind event planning, and should be mandatory reading for planners everywhere."
—*Leslie McNabb, Senior Manager Event Planning, Scotia Capital*

EVENT PLANNING ETHICS AND ETIQUETTE

A Principled Approach to the Business of Special Event Management

(ISBN: 978-0-470-83260-8)

"This is a must-read not only for event professionals, but also for small-business people conceiving product introductions and conference appearances."
—*Harvard Business School, Working Knowledge*

"An excellent, timely benchmark for all of those who strive to achieve the highest standard in the event planning industry."
—*Marta Pawych, CMM, CMP, CSEP; Director Meetings, Events & Sponsorships, Human Resources Professionals Association of Ontario*

"Judy Allen strikes again. The veteran event planner...writes with the voice of experience and offers readers guidelines for establishing ethical policies in the office and on-site at events...a good refresher, and an excellent reading for novices who need to know how to keep personal and professional boundaries from being crossed."
—*Corporate Meetings & Incentives Magazine*

"This book contains invaluable information for anyone who handles events for their organization. A host of real-world stories from the field—the good, the bad, and the ugly—serve as examples of codes of conduct (or lack thereof) as well as cautionary tales of what can happen when ethics and etiquette fall to the wayside. Allen thoroughly examines many scenarios and provides practical advice that any planner would be foolish not to heed."
—*Charity Village*

TIME MANAGEMENT FOR EVENT PLANNERS

Expert Techniques and Time-Saving Tips for Organizing Your Workload, Prioritizing Your Day, and Taking Control of Your Schedule

(ISBN: 978-0-470-83626-2)

"She has done it again! Judy Allen has written an excellent, educational and user-friendly book, which is a priceless resource for planners worldwide. "
—*Ysabelle Allard, Meetings & Incentives Planner, Bilingual Meetings & Incentives*

"At last, a time management book written by someone who knows what it is to juggle three programs, six clients, eighteen suppliers and a family in a pear tree! Using Judy Allen's tips have really made a difference!"
—*Brigitte Mondor, CMP, Event Leader, Microsoft—Maritz Canada Inc.*

"A very no-nonsense approach to the real problem of time management. Some excellent tips and strategies for the busy professional."
—*Deborah Breiter, Associate Professor, Rosen College of Hospitality, Orlando, Florida*

"Time is money, and organizing your time is the key to planning a successful event. Judy Allen's new book gives event planners all the tools they need to manage their time most efficiently."
—*Luis R. Rodriguez, Executive President (CEO), International Standardization, for the Meeting Industry Institute (ISMI), Isla Margarita, Venezuela*

"In this practical skills-based text, Judy Allen explores time management and provides techniques for event professionals to learn and apply to your work. From exploring your current use of time, through prioritising and action planning, to multi tasking, project management and balancing your personal and professional life, Judy provides hints and tips for making better, and the best, use of time, based on her years of experience in the events industry."
—*Glenn A. J. Bowdin, Principal Lecturer, UK Centre for Events Management, Leeds Metropolitan University*

THE EXECUTIVE'S GUIDE TO CORPORATE EVENTS AND BUSINESS ENTERTAINING

How to Choose and Use Company Functions to Increase Brand Awareness, Develop New Business, Nurture Customer Loyalty and Drive Growth

(ISBN: 978-0-470-83848-8)

"A goldmine of insight and instruction. Anyone planning any type of business event, large or small, must have a copy of this book!"
—*Lisa K. Altizer, Marketing Director, Mercer Mall, West Virginia*

"As usual, Judy Allen has written a valuable book filled with important information. She adds depth and breadth to the body of practical knowledge about the nuts and bolts of event strategy and tactics. This volume should at all times be on the desk of every planner and every business executive charged with planning an event."
—*David Sorin, Esq., CEO, Management Mpowerment Associates, and Author of* The Special Events Advisor: A Business and Legal Guide for Event Professionals

"Intelligent planning and thorough execution are the keys to success for any corporate function. Judy Allen outlines a succinct, practical methodology that will ensure your next event achieves its stated business objectives and creates a positive lasting impression."
—*Zeke Adkins, Co-founder, Luggage Forward*

"In today's competitive business climate, a 'business as usual' approach to corporate events and functions simply does not work. Judy Allen has compiled in one comprehensive guide everything today's successful executive needs to know to take this strategic function to the next level."
—*Evans Gebhardt, Executive Vice President, Eos Airlines, Inc.*

MARKETING YOUR
event planning
BUSINESS

A Creative Approach to
Gaining the Competitive Edge

JUDY ALLEN

John Wiley & Sons Canada, Ltd.

Library and Archives Canada Cataloguing in Publication Data
Allen, Judy, 1952-
    Marketing your event planning business : a creative approach
to gaining the competitive edge / Judy Allen

Includes index.
ISBN 0-470-83387-4
ISBN 978-1-118-51445-0 (pbk)

    1. Special events industry—Marketing. I. Title.

GT3405.A46 2004   394.2'0688   C2004-901562-1

Production Credits
Cover design & interior text design: Interrobang Graphic Design Inc.
Printer: Hume Intermedia Inc.

John Wiley & Sons Canada, Ltd.
6045 Freemont Blvd.
Mississauga, Ontario
L5R 4J3

1 2 3 4 5 HI 17 16 15 14 13

Dedication

This book is dedicated to the millions of people whose job it is to sell themselves and their business everyday. Those who are top in their field know firsthand the value of doing visibility well and challenge themselves daily to master new marketing techniques, become more innovative in soliciting sales, develop areas of specialization, create niche markets and pursue new clients. They continually strive to find ways to create fresh opportunities for success, set themselves apart from their competition, capture their clients' attention and gain the competitive edge. One sale at a time, through their marketing efforts, they position themselves to transform not only the quality of their lives, but also the lives of those they work for and with.

CONTENTS

ACKNOWLEDGMENTS

Writing and releasing four Event Planning books, in four years, has meant working closely with a great team of professionals at John Wiley and Sons. I would like to thank Robert Harris, General Manager; Karen Milner, Executive Editor; Elizabeth McCurdy, Project Manager; Robert Hickey, Project Coordinator; Jennifer Smith, Director of Sales and Marketing; Meghan Brousseau, Publicist; Lucas Wilk, Associate Channel Marketing Manager; Kari Romaniuk, Channel Marketing Manager; Parisa Michail, Corporate Account Manager; Joan Trinidad, Accountant; Karen Bryan, Publishing Service Director; and Christine Rae, Designer for the very special part they have played in creating a series of books that have been warmly embraced by readers, reviewers, colleges and universities around the world.

Daphne Hart, my literary agent, Helen Heller Agency Inc., represents her clients with professionalism and grace. I value her guidance and enjoy working closely with her on what has turned out to be an amazing journey. Thanks Daphne for sharing your expertise with me. Once again, I would also like to thank Helen Heller, for her assistance.

Working with Ron Edward, Focus Strategic Communications and Michelle Bullard on the structure and copy edit of this book has proven to be as enlightening an experience as always. Thank you both for the important part you play in turning manuscripts into successful books.

I would like to thank all of the reviewers, who took the time to read my books and bring their valuable insight to readers. I am very grateful for your endorsements. Your kind words were very much appreciated and I take your words to heart.

I have received hundreds of e-mails and telephone calls from readers and your words are very meaningful to me. I did not set out to write a series of books on event planning. I wrote the fist book to act as a guide and provide a strong foundation in event planning. The comments, questions and thank you's I received from readers, enabled me to see what industry issues still needed to be addressed. There were common threads in the messages and I paid attention to what was being asked. The second book was written in direct response to the requests I received, and that book led to the third, which in turn produced the fourth. Thank you all for the very valuable part you played in bringing about this newest endeavor.

And as always, I would like to thank my family, my parents Walter and Ruth, my sister, Marilyn, my nieces Natasha and Jasmine, Hans, Blair, my extended family, and my friends for their love and support.

PREFACE

In the wake of September 11, and with the ongoing turmoil in world events and the economy, the event planning industry has been hit hard. In what was already a highly competitive industry, many planners and companies are struggling to survive. September 11, 2001 stopped travel and event planning in its tracks, as the terrorist attacks brought about an initial fear of flying, which resulted in corporations immediately calling off out-of-country and out-of-state events. These cancellations and the subsequent loss of revenue affected everyone in the hospitality industry. A number of meetings, conferences and special events were shifted to locations closer to home to lessen corporate and attendee anxiety. Venue requirements for events changed, towering buildings were ruled out—as were high-profile sites—and companies began to conduct more business meetings via conference call or Webcast as opposed to face to face.

Next to impact the event planning world was tumbling stock markets. This was followed by white-collar crime that had corporate CEOs and company executives making national headlines with their irresponsible spending and lack of ethical behavior. Companies were being brought down and often the consequence was massive employee layoffs. Money for event planning became tight. Large corporations that had held large events in the past no longer could. After all, when employees are being laid off, it is difficult to justify any expense that could be deemed unnecessary. Company spending was held under a magnifying glass by remaining employees and stockholders. And this was only the beginning.

What came next were the wars in Afghanistan and Iraq, ongoing terrorist attacks around the world, mysterious cruise line illnesses, sniper attacks in the U.S., airline bankruptcies, West Nile virus, mad cow disease, SARS and even monkeypox. Destinations once deemed safe from terrorism and illness became *verboten*, having an economic impact on not just the event planning and hospitality field but on seemingly unrelated businesses such as the farming and fishing industries. For example, if restaurants and hotel rooms were not being filled, those who earned their living supplying, manufacturing and delivering specialty food and beverage items that may have been flown, shipped or trucked in daily—such as lobsters from Maine, crab cakes from Maryland, potatoes from P.E.I., liquor and fruit drinks from exotic locales—were being financially hurt as well. Not only were hotels and restaurants sitting empty, theaters in major cities went dark with shows closing up when they could no longer fill seats. And to top it all off, major cities suffered legendary blackouts, such as the one in the summer of 2003 on the eastern seaboard of North America, and even countries such as Italy were shut down for up to a week. Then there were hurricanes, floods and major earthquakes that those planning events had to grapple with. *And all of this took place within the span of two years.*

Each one of these developments had an immediate domino effect on the hospitality industry that was felt around the world and forever changed the way event planning business would be conducted in the future. Trusted suppliers, seemingly far removed from what were deemed problem locations, were on the verge of going under, and layoffs were imminent as the financial impact of cancellations and loss of business rippled through the industry. Airlines took away commissions they had been paying planners. Hoteliers, suppliers and destination management companies began to go head-to-head, competing with event planners for business. Event planning companies had to re-group, re-organize and re-strategize. Organizations and individuals in the event planning and hospitality industry that had not prepared to weather a force majeure went under. The ones who remained found themselves looking at a much smaller pie, still to be divided among many players. While some had disappeared, there was still a lot of competition as some suppliers sought to become their replacement. Their goal was to have clients deal with them direct, as opposed to working through the event planning company, and reduce or cut out the role the event planners played in order to increase their profit share. Past working partnerships and business alliances went by the wayside as each side hurried to stake out their claim on potential clients.

The question being asked today is how to thrive—as both an individual and a company—and not merely survive in this new era of free market conditions. The event planning industry as a whole has learned that it is no longer enough to just plan and prepare for the next series of events. Planners themselves must be ready for the unexpected if they want to be in a strong position to ride out any future economic slumps and still be in business tomorrow. For example, in December of 2003 another case of mad cow disease struck again and brought the beef industry in the U.S. and Canada to an immediate halt, with billions of import dollars at stake as countries around the world banned their beef from being brought in. Right on its heels came news of another suspected SARS case. Still unprepared for this re-occurrence, the cattle industry was thrown into a frenzy about how to recoup losses, how to get through this period of time and what they can do in future to avoid the same thing from happening again. Had laws in the U.S. been passed making it illegal to slaughter downer animals (those too sick to stand) after the first case appeared in Canada, the meat from this cow would not have gotten into the food system and caused a panic when it was discovered that beef from the infected cow had been sent to eight states and Guam. This finding also had an immediate effect on the event planning industry, as clients and their guests once again began to question food and destination safety. Businesses must become proactive, anticipating and preparing to circumvent the worst-case scenario from happening again, instead of sitting back and reacting, scrambling for solutions, when disaster strikes. The end result of this second occurrence with tainted meat resulted in tougher U.S. controls being brought in to match tighter Canadian laws to prevent downer cows from entering the food chain. Had this ruling taken place immediately after the first mad cow scare, the North American cattle industry and the world's beef consumers would not have been placed in financial jeopardy and at a perceived health risk.

Planners, suppliers and event planning companies know now that if they resist change, they could cease to exist. They know that those who are embracing the challenge now before the event planning industry are intent on moving forward quickly, focused on securing as big a piece of the business pie for themselves as they can, actively seeking solutions that will allow them to conduct and manage their current accounts better, and looking for new ways to move to the forefront in creating new business opportunities where seemingly none may have existed before.

This book shows event planners, event planning management companies, suppliers and their clients how to gain the competitive edge by setting themselves apart, pursuing new markets and soliciting new sales. Comprehensive coverage in this book includes how to diversify your client base; how to develop niche markets and areas of expertise; defining and customizing customer service; how to establish a business backup plan to defend against downturns in business; how to develop innovative ideas for soliciting sales; and how and when to set up your own event planning business.

Marketing Your Event Planning Business: A Creative Approach to Gaining the Competitive Edge discusses creative new ways for planners, suppliers and event planning companies to showcase their talents, build their business and bring added value to their clients. As an industry, event planning crosses many disciplines, and a successful planner must have, along with event design and management skills, an in-depth knowledge of accounting, business and law. One key area that has long been overlooked is marketing. Event planners know and understand event marketing, but they must learn how to market themselves and their companies to gain the competitive edge in the event planning business.

This book covers three key marketing areas: marketability, market development and marketing endeavors. Part One of this book examines ways of making yourself and your company marketable; the importance of acquiring areas of expertise; how to create your personal niche; and the value of niche marketing. For example, not every tenting company has expertise in converting a swimming pool into a dance floor or dining area. For some clients, this is becoming a "must do" for their next event, and it is not inexpensive, easily earning the tenting company more than US$20,000. So, it is a worthwhile skill to develop. One tenting company that excels in this has an employee who is renowned for his success in this area and is booked nonstop. He acquired an area of expertise that is needed and he developed it into his niche. There are few that can do what he does, and event planning companies know that if they book that particular company they do not have to worry about the pool being damaged in the covering process or that the guests will take an unexpected dip in the pool while dining or dancing. Acquiring this area of expertise was important; it helped the employee become known in his field and very marketable, and his knowledge enabled the tenting company he worked for to gain a competitive edge in a profitable market.

Part Two explores market development, which includes how to define your company objectives and identify exactly who your client is. How to target your talents is also reviewed. Targeting your talents means focusing your energies where they will be most successful and on clients that are most desirable. In the above example, the tenting company targeted its talents to clients who had the dollars, who were looking to create special effects and whose guests were likely to be able to afford its services. Its skills became well known in high society, by those attending events it had done. When a major fashion designer was looking for someone to tent its upcoming fashion show extravaganza, it turned to this company and brought it in from out of the country to handle its event. There was no one locally whose work it considered up to par. The tenting company had targeted its talents to the right customer profile, and in the time when money was tight it still had more business than it could handle.

Part Two also shows you how to understand and customize your customer service requirements. Not all customer services needs are the same. The days of schmoozing are past. People's priorities have changed. Customized customer service is what is being required. For instance, a team of successful lawyers (laid off due to recent company downsizing) came together to provide a service where the lawyer will come to your business or home at a time most convenient to you. They understood that for the clients they were seeking, cost was not a factor. Convenience was what their customers were looking for. They saw a need, filled it and business is booming. Ways to define and customize customer service are also discussed in this book. Lengthy business lunches no longer hold appeal—not if they're going to impact meeting a deadline or end up taking personal time away at the end of the day. People want to socialize with family and friends and pursue individual interests, as opposed to spending time with business acquaintances or those looking to solicit their business over lunch.

Part Three looks into marketing endeavors and ways to market to your audience, innovative ways on how to solicit sales, and the value of diversification. Event planning companies that have not learned the value of diversifying were greatly affected by recent events. North American companies that specialized only in exotic travel destinations had to scramble when businesses wanted to hold events closer to home. Those event planning companies did not have a business backup plan. They lost lead time trying to recover and to establish themselves as experts in North American facilities. Their focus was too narrow. They never diversified or prepared for the unexpected, and consequently many had to lay off staff. Hotels that catered only to the luxury individual traveler sat empty when the stock market and their clients' personal incomes fell. Hotels that had diversified were not hit as hard. Their creative marketing endeavors ensured that they still had bread-and-butter income coming in where others had nothing. Now more than ever, companies that learn to diversify will succeed in gaining the competitive edge. We will see some of the ways to do so in this book.

Part Three also covers when individuals should go out on their own. For many involved in event planning there comes a time when the prospect of setting up their own company becomes appealing. The costs and benefits of doing so will be made clear. Some individuals may be better off working for an employer as a sales representative or account executive, but others may want to explore other options. The pluses and minus of each will be detailed.

This book will be of value to the professional event planner, suppliers, clients who are hiring and working with professional planners and suppliers, as well as those in related industries.

PART 1

Marketability

The first three chapters of this book look at the importance of marketability—for individuals and for companies—in the event planning industry. Marketability is often defined as having marketable goods, services or skills that are in demand and that meet a specific need. Having marketability applies equally to individuals, companies, products or services. People who take steps to ensure that they have appeal increase their chances of a successful and financially rewarding career. They are the ones who stand out as stars in their industry, that are actively pursued on the job front and are continually being hired up. Companies want to hire individuals who will in turn enhance their firm's own marketability to its customers. Bringing marketable employees onboard becomes an investment to the employer and is viewed as a means of making the company more attractive to future clients, as well as giving it an advantage over its competition.

In today's market, an employee who has marketability is an important commodity to any employer. Companies are hiring not only the individual's knowledge, skills and experience, but their personality and reputation as well. They know the value that acquiring a set of sought-after skills brings to their clients and how it can raise their company's profile and their profits. Companies that are never-ending in their pursuit of improving their marketability are ensuring their competitive edge in business at all times. People want to do business with those who are current, knowledgeable and growing in the right direction. Ways to make yourself and your company marketable are outlined in the first chapter.

Developing areas of expertise adds to the marketability of an individual and a business, so ways to do this are reviewed in Chapter 2. Many event planning industry leaders attribute their success to having acquired expertise in specialty fields, as well as having mastered other key business elements that worked to propel them forward professionally. Not being proficient in certain areas can leave you sitting on the sidelines. Knowing which will take you further fastest can make a big difference in your career.

To stand out from your competition, you need to find a special area of demand for a product or service that only you can fulfill. In an industry where everyone is now competing for the same bit of business, what will set you apart? It is the ability to offer something unique to potential employers or customers. You can tailor your niche to fit your consumer audience by determining what is new and would be compelling to them. Niche marketing is a simple concept that can help individuals or businesses gain an advantage over their competitors. Ways to create your niche in the event planning industry are discussed in Chapter 3.

1
MAKING YOURSELF MARKETABLE

The professional meeting, incentive and special event industry is growing and attracting more and more aspiring planners each day. Universities and colleges worldwide are now offering courses and accreditation, and many are fostering an entrepreneurial spirit, developing graduates set on opening and operating their own businesses immediately. The competition for jobs in the workforce and to contract new clients has never been more intense. Almost daily, new companies are opening their doors for business, and those applying new business practices are experiencing tremendous success. Enterprising independent meeting planners are winning accounts away from long-established meeting planning companies and incentive houses. Some of the industry's biggest players are laying off employees and even closing their doors, while smaller specialty boutique operations are thriving. How did this industry turnabout happen? Those who are moving forward placed their focus on increasing their marketability and investing in themselves and their companies, while those who are experiencing financial hardships are more likely the ones who have persisted in clinging to old ways of soliciting business.

The question that planners and event planning companies are asking themselves is how they can stand out from the crowd, maintain old clients and attract new business opportunities. Doing all you can to make yourself extremely marketable is one of the most effective ways. In business, your knowledge, personality and reputation are what makes you marketable, both as an individual and as a company.

There are three key steps to making you and your company marketable:

1. Target Your Talents: Never stop investing in yourself.

2. Distinguish Yourself and Your Company: Showcase your expertise by becoming visible. Learn how to build public awareness by using industry network and media effectively so that you can position yourself for success.

3. Manage Your Reputation: Watch out for your personal and professional reputation and be protective of your good name.

TARGET YOUR TALENTS

In the past, event planning was a field that many just fell into. There was little offered in the way of formal education and training and most of what was available was through industry associations. There were very few books on the subject and people were not very open about sharing information. It was an industry where you learned by trial and error, from being on familiarization trips, taking part in site inspections, and handling an event on site. In the late 1980s many of today's leading event planning companies were still receiving supplier quotes on telex machines, and preparing cost summaries manually, using adding machines and typewriters. Fax machines were embraced when they were first introduced, but in some offices the single, shared computers sat gathering dust as people clung to the old comfortable way of doing business.

Immersed in the day-to-day drama of event planning, deadlines and intense work demands, many planners left continuing education up to their employers. Owners faced a dilemma when it came to deciding whether or not to invest in employee education. The fear of time and money spent had to be weighed against the possibility of employees leaving, taking with them their newly acquired skills and having someone else be the benefactor. Some owners were so paranoid that they would not let their employees out of the office for familiarization trips or presentations for fear that they would meet someone who would lure them away. Many owners chose to do nothing. And they discovered what happens when you don't invest in growing your company and your employees. They became stagnant, lost their momentum, and in the process suffered loss of business and standing in the event planning community.

Today, planners are taking responsibility for ongoing education and investing in themselves. Planners know that enlightened companies are now hiring with an eye on industry experience, knowledge, areas of expertise and accreditation. Some would-be planners start out to set themselves apart from their job-seeking peers by successfully completing industry courses that will allow them to receive certification once they have been hired and have completed the certificate's work hour requirements.

They know investing in education can give you:

- Professional credibility
- Expertise
- Special recognition
- Prestige and industry reputation
- Competitive advantage in securing a position or soliciting business
- Marketability
- Promotions
- Increased earning potential

Those dedicated to investing in themselves and increasing their marketability are making the time to better their skills and are committing to being leaders in their industry by taking every available opportunity to upgrade their learning. The meeting, incentive and special event planning industry offers an abundance of educational resources, including:

- Formal Education
- Industry Certification
- Associations
- Professional Resources (Books/Magazines/Online Publications)

- Industry Conferences, Congresses, Trade Shows and Award Shows

FORMAL EDUCATION

Formal education can pay dividends for the rest of your life. Studies show that graduates of colleges, universities and technical institutes can earn hundreds of thousands of dollars more over their career than can non-graduates. Planners already in the industry who know the difference a degree can make are going back to school as mature students and signing up for courses that have opened up in the event planning field. Others are embracing distance learning as the perfect solution, preferring to learn online at their own pace. For those who are wondering how they can fit further education development into their busy schedule—when there is not enough time in their day for personal, family and professional demands *and* a commute to classes—this is a viable option. There are a variety of opportunities out there for distance education in the event planning field. For example, one North American planner just completed her master's degree in tourism management from a university in Australia without setting foot on the campus.

INDUSTRY CERTIFICATION

Industry certification also increases earning potential. Those with industry certification, such as Certified Meeting Professionals (CMPs), can earn up to US$10,000 more annually than non-CMPs. The more knowledge and skills you can accumulate in the event planning industry, the more valuable you become. Industry standards have been set, and those who meet them are in demand. In this challenging industry, you continue to grow and expand your understanding through experience and professional development. With proper training, event planning can be developed into an art form.

Samples of internationally recognized event planning industry certification include:

- Certified in Exhibition Management (CEM)
- Certified Incentive Travel Executive (CITE)
- Certified Manager of Exhibits (CME)
- Global Certification in Meeting Management (CMM)
- Certified Meeting Professional (CMP)

- Certified Special Events Professional (CSEP)

Certification eligibility, the qualification process and contact information to become certifiable for each of the industry designations listed above can be found in Appendix A of this book.

ASSOCIATIONS

When you are starting out in the event planning field, joining an association is a good first step. Membership in an association serves as a means to introduce you to the industry, meet your peers and learn more about your chosen profession. It is also a way to become actively involved and to start making a name for yourself in the event planning community. You can begin by attending meetings, and progress by volunteering and serving on various committees and even running for a seat on the board of directors. Each step helps you move forward in becoming known in the industry and being involved keeps you on top of changes that are taking place. You may even end up being instrumental in setting new standards.

T I P	Although it may be tempting to sit with those you know at industry events, there is more value in moving outside your comfort zone and introducing yourself to those you have not met. Too often, planners don't practice what they teach their clients—get your guests circulating—and remain in their select clusters, losing a valuable marketing opportunity in the process by not moving outside their immediate circle of business acquaintances. You never know who else may be in the room, who knows who, who can introduce you to someone that you have been wanting to meet or who may be in a position to sing your praises to an important business contact—unless you take steps to expand your business network.

Being part of an association enables planners to network with local and international peers; be apprised of breaking industry news; take part in educational conferences, seminars, certification and leadership programs; and stay on top of latest trends and issues affecting the industry.

Important industry associations and councils, many of which have worldwide chapters, include:

- CIC—Convention Industry Council
- CSES—Canadian Special Events Society
- HSMAI—Hospitality Sales and Marketing Association International
- IAAP—International Association of Administrative Professionals
- IACC—International Association of Conference Centers
- IAEM—International Association for Exhibition Management
- IMPAC—Independent Meeting Planners Association of Canada, Inc.
- ISES—International Special Events Society
- MPI—Meeting Professionals International
- NACE—National Association of Catering Executives
- PCMA—Professional Convention Management Association
- SCMP—Society of Corporate Meeting Professionals
- SITE—The Society of Incentive & Travel Executives

Contact and general information for each of the associations listed above can be found in Appendix B of this book.

PROFESSIONAL RESOURCES (BOOKS/MAGAZINES/ONLINE PUBLICATIONS)

It is essential in the fast-paced, ever-changing world of event planning to keep yourself current. One way of doing this is by subscribing to industry magazines, and purchasing event planning books and best-selling books on business, current affairs, marketing, public relations, party planning and entertaining. Online publications such as *BiZBash*, *Chief Marketer* and *MIMlist* are other excellent resources (MIMlist Meeting Matters is the meetings industry's leading e-mail-based discussion group, where you can participate in conversations with more than 2,000 of your industry peers).

Magazines, books and online publications offer ideas, tips and information on coming trends and successful techniques that can be adapted to meet your individual event planning needs. Use them as teaching tools and sources of information, innovation and inspiration. Seeing or reading about a new product or idea may be just the trigger you need to come up with a fabulous new party theme or introduce an exciting new element to your event.

A wealth of industry information can be found at your fingertips online (online publications), in your e-blasts (marketing e-mails) and through your e-newsletters (industry/association newsletters), as well as through regular mail (magazine subscriptions) and through association bookstores. You can find relevant books through Amazon, Barnes and Noble and Chapters.Indigo, and have them delivered right to your home or office.

Meeting planning, incentives and event planning are always in transition. Planners must be skilled at reading upcoming trends, keeping on top of industry rules and regulations and predicting the next hot destination venue or theme. Industry knowledge and continuing education is of paramount importance. It is what will set you and the company you work with apart from the herd.

A sample listing of professional industry resources can be found in Appendix C of this book.

INDUSTRY CONFERENCES, CONGRESSES, TRADE SHOWS AND AWARD SHOWS

You can further your education by attending local, national and world conferences, congresses, trade shows and award shows. Be sure to take advantage of the wealth of information that is made available to you by the event planning industry. When you attend seminars given by industry leaders, you can come away with information that you can immediately put to use, because they know the issues that are facing you back in the office. Attending educational symposiums can also teach you how to run an event. You will see firsthand the different operating styles and get immediate feedback of what to do and what not to do at your next event. If those planning the event miss a step, they will no doubt hear about it and get to witness in person the crowd's reaction. At one premier event planning award show, the company doing the centerpieces made a major mistake and had displays set up at each table that, while impressive, no one could see over, around or through once seated. The audience—seasoned event planning pros—immediately removed theirs from the table.

At another event, mashed potatoes served in a martini glass as a trendy appetizer remained untouched, with guests unwilling to consume so many carbs on what to them were merely basic potatoes and too heavy considering a full dinner was following. One seminar onboard a boat had guests longing to be rescued when the electricity died. That affected many of the evening's components, from food preparation and air conditioning to music and even the operation of the toilets. Seeing what can go wrong and how teams of industry experts implement crisis management is perhaps even a greater learning experience than taking part in a perfectly executed event.

You also get to observe how different venues operate. This is especially useful if you are attending an event at a property that you may have considered in the past but not had the opportunity to use as yet. You may also get to see cutting-edge technology at work, as the newest ideas are often on display at industry events. For example, different online and on-site registration systems may be being tested.

Some of the industry's well-known conferences, congresses, trade shows and award shows, along with contact information, can be found in Appendix D of this book.

DISTINGUISH YOURSELF AND YOUR COMPANY

Event planning companies looking to make themselves marketable to employees—in order to attract the best in the business to work for them—know the value of showcasing what they have to offer. They understand that this is not just a marketing application designed to bring in potential customers. When employers have the best minds in the business working for them, they know they are giving themselves the competitive edge of added marketability, and they do this by distinguishing themselves from their competition. They play up their differences publicly.

In the past, event planning owners seemed to look for employees who worked ceaselessly to meet the demands of their business. Their employees would work past exhaustion to meet deadlines, sometimes even crashing on the company floor to sleep for a couple of hours before beginning again. Employers are no longer looking for that. They know that having an employee who is out of balance will eventually lead to poor productivity and burnout. Managing business wants without jeopardizing personal and professional needs is becoming very important to employers, employees and customers. Flexible hours and working from home are now viable options some employers will consider if it means they can secure a talented employee.

Many companies are adding well-being centers to their office areas, where employees can go to meditate, catch a power nap, or take a shower. Some companies are even installing gyms and hiring personal trainers to lead their staff in yoga classes and provide personal fitness training, all in an effort to help employees relieve some of the stress of their day, and ultimately to increase effectual productivity and to attract highly marketable employees to work for them. Others provide complimentary bottled water and wholesome snacks, or go so far as to set up juice bars, to make sure their employees are never running on empty or trying to sustaining themselves on caffeine and junk food, especially in crunch periods. One company turned its boardroom into a screening room and brought in movies to help stimulate innovative ideas and creative discussion. Another installed a personal spa so employees could get haircuts, massages, manicures and other pampering during their lunch hours. It provided an oasis of calm, and made personal self-care easy so that employees could fully focus on the job at hand, make better decisions and improve their performance and customer service.

These employers are fully behind their employees meeting deadlines while meeting their personal and professional needs, going home on time to be with family and friends or being able to attend industry functions and classes. Living a life in balance, and being given the tools to do so are moving to the forefront and working with a business to create new energy and creativity. Employers know that if their employees are not given time to acquire areas of expertise and to target their talents, they and the company grow stagnant. A revolving door is the end result—and time and money is spent on retraining as opposed to building an unbeatable team to take the company forward. Companies looking to give themselves the competitive edge want the brightest minds working for them, not their competition.

Some media-savvy companies make sure to plant stories in industry publications and local newspapers that highlight how well their employees and customers are cared for. They submit story ideas; invite the media into their offices to see them at work, cover an event or take part in a charity event such as a golf tournament; and make sure that areas of appeal are photographed and talked about in the article. They know the old saying that a picture is worth a thousand words has merit. If their purpose is creating an opportunity to entice people to work for them and potential clients to do business with them, then great care is taken with the photo op setup. What they are selling is their brand, and it is important that it is projected in all they do. They are presenting to the public the image they want seen and nothing is left to chance. For example, at the charity event, they will make sure that their donation is presented on an oversized check with their company name clearly visible, and that a photographer is there to capture the moment, even if they have to supply their own professional photographer in order to get the exact pictures they want to convey their message. That way they are in control of the prints and can send out copies to magazines and newspapers that may be interested in running the story and photographs, showing their company giving back to the community and supporting local charities.

They know that a photo is a marketing tool that can be used to convey a message. It can effectively be used to put forth a feeling. For example, a company wishing to convey a casual, relaxed working atmosphere may wish to have the individuals in a picture appear less formal—without ties, with collars left unbuttoned and shirt sleeves rolled up or perhaps a sport jackets rather than suits and more formal business attire. And this applies not only to those whose picture is being taken but anyone who could be conceivably captured in the background. If you see a photograph in the newspaper of a company executive leaning back in his chair, on the telephone with his feet up on the desk, it is done by design; it is not an off-guard moment in the life of a busy VIP. Even the shoes propped up on the desk will have been orchestrated. If you look closely you will probably see that the soles are unmarked, and the shoes, most likely designer brands to discreetly convey affluence, that his company is doing well and that the employees are well paid, were most probably brought in for the occasion.

Final picture and story content approval is often asked for as well, with the company citing that this is being done at the request of its company lawyers, as it is important to maintain control of what is being put out to the public. And it wants the picture and the story to convey as much as possible of the image it wants to showcase. Names and titles of individuals appearing in the picture are also supplied so there is no room for error, and the company name is provided exactly as the company wishes it to be listed. It wants to capitalize on self-promotion and have potential clients, employees and suppliers recognize it and be able to find it. It uses these same techniques in its advertising and company promotions. And many are starting to turn to the pros, hiring public relations companies to help them achieve their goals.

Along with public relations companies, executives in the public eye are now hiring speechwriters in order to give more polished presentations, even for what could be perceived to be informal gatherings. They don't want to miss an opportunity to enhance their professional image no matter how insignificant an event may seem to be. It is a tactic long used by those whose intention is to shine in the limelight and maximize their exposure. U.S. presidents who have needed to impart a touch of humor in their speeches to the public have taken it one step further, hiring professional joke writers in addition to having their personal staff writers. Heads of companies use this same method when preparing for their speaking engagements. If they want to come across as warm and caring with amusing anecdotes to share, when they are in fact uncomfortable speaking in public, they bring in the experts to work with them and to put them at ease. This is often done on the advice of their event planning company. Event planners are now taking their own advice. They know if they want a competitive edge in business they have to move from backstage to centerstage at times, and when they do so they need to radiate confidence.

Individuals in all industries who wish to put themselves forward and distinguish themselves from their peers have used the same strategies to market their expertise and their talents. They know that becoming "visible" in the industry can boost their career opportunities. They care about how they present themselves in and out of the office, whether on familiarization trips or site inspections, at industry functions or attending their clients' programs. They don't ever want their name associated with being a "guest gone wild" at a professional get-together. That is not a desirable way of becoming part of the industry buzz. They keep their professional demeanor in check and their personal life private, and they manage to do it without being stuffy.

People who are looking to make a name for themselves in the industry will take the time to pose for pictures at industry functions; they'll be available to be quoted as an industry source for newspaper and magazine articles; they'll join associations and volunteer to sit on boards; they'll head up committees or help out at the next get-together; and they'll work the registration desk at educational seminars, getting to meet people face to face and put names to faces. Then when their duties are over they are free to mix and mingle with key individuals they know firsthand are in the room. If there are speakers of note attending, keen individuals will volunteer to look after them, taking the opportunity to find out before the event if they have any special needs and chat with them. They will make it a point to work in some one-on-one time with them. They will volunteer to facilitate meetings and do onstage introductions. If they have specific talents they make sure they are known and step in where their expertise is needed, and if they can work in a thank you credit in promotional material they can add that to their portfolio.

Today, along with a good resume, you also need good marketing. You need to play up your credentials and use the media and your marketability effectively. The goal is to expand your demand and to build your personal brand.

Consider an up-and-coming sports figure who wanted to become a household name. Though just starting out he knew the value of good PR and hired a public relations company to help him get media attention. Cheering "fans," dressed in a manner that would attract television and newspaper cameras, as well as signs showcasing the player's name, were planted in the stands. The money was well spent, as the hired fans made the six o'clock news and the front page of the sports section. Although the player had bought his own hype, people bought into it as well. He had accomplished what he had set out to do—become visible.

Many event planners have hired the equivalent of cheering fans when doing theme parties such as Oscar night parties or events for corporate clients, but they would not think about how to use the same techniques to make themselves stand out. One employee in search of a job decided to use his creativity to market himself. He delivered a teaser mailing to prospective employers. This consisted of a glass container filled with gold flakes with a message attached that said this individual was worth his weight in gold. He received a number of callbacks for interviews and several job offers. What he was selling was not only himself but also his creativity. The cost was minimal but the gimmick maximized the possibility that someone would notice his resume. Another employee on a job hunt took visibility and making herself distinctive a step further. She took out a billboard posting her picture, qualifications and expected salary, which was in the six figures. She received over 120 responses. She got both the dream job she was seeking and the expected salary, which more than paid for the cost of the billboard.

Use the creativity you bring to event planning to look for ways to market yourself. Don't shy away from publicity. Look for chances to demonstrate your talents and create them if need be. Distinguish yourself from your peers by marketing yourself in a positive light and making sure that you do "visibility" as well as you do event planning.

Companies and individuals have the opportunity to display their professional image, expertise and talents at:

- Supplier presentations
- Educational seminars
- Association meetings
- Conferences
- Trade shows
- Industry functions (e.g., charity golf tournaments)
- Client presentation meetings
- Supplier meetings
- Familiarization trips
- Site inspections
- On-site event orchestration
- In the office
- On an airplane
- In a hotel
- Everyday out and about

> **T**
> **I**
> **P**
>
> Never lose sight of the fact that you don't know who may be sitting beside you when you are going about your day-to-day activities, and opportunities to put yourself forward could happen when least expected. One planner, on an aircraft that was experiencing mechanical problems and landing at the nearest airport, called the office while she was still airborne to re-route and book an alternate flight. She knew there would be a crush at the airport when they arrived, with passengers scrambling to find other flights to their final destination. She offered to assist the person seated beside her with his plans, not knowing that he was

the CEO of a major corporation that most event planning companies would love to call their client. This passenger was so impressed that he asked for her card, called her when he returned from business and invited her company to come in and present personally to him at his next executive meeting. They were awarded the business. An accidental meeting, when someone was given a chance to showcase her talents, turned into a profitable and lasting business relationship.

MANAGE YOUR REPUTATION

Your reputation is your industry credibility, and yes, there are such things as good publicity and bad publicity. What happens when an individual or a company does something wrong and attracts negative press?

People are distrustful of doing business with those they think are trying to put a spin on the facts and they feel are trying to cover up those facts. The situation is often immediately diffused if there is a sense of ownership, a mea culpa followed by immediate action taken to right a wrong. When it was reported in the media that an airline had violated its own privacy regulations and divulged confidential customer information to a third party, the company head immediately took responsibility, explained why and how this had occurred and described the steps that were in place to make sure that it never happened again. It turned out that an official request had been made for disclosure of confidential passenger information, such as customers' names, addresses, telephone numbers, credit card numbers, flights they had booked, and who they were traveling with, to see how this type of information could be compiled and used to aid national security. The third party in this case was not going to use the actual information it received. The furor died down after a couple of days. The airline that made headlines had an outstanding record of customer service, and while confidence had been shaken, customers valued hearing the truth.

There are always going to be petty people who will bring up incidents or bad behavior years after the fact in an attempt to demean and belittle others or sway business their way. People make mistakes. Events sometimes spiral out of control. It is how these situations are handled that should be looked at. Were they dealt with with truth and transparency, or was the idea of damage control to sweep everything under the carpet? What should be called into question is the behavior of the people making the disparaging remarks and their lack of professional ethics.

Employers and clients are looking for those who can set trends, not just follow them. Those who are on top of their game and professional in their behavior will be in demand. Clients and employers will seek out those who know what has been done in the industry and what can be done, and those who have the imagination and skills to create something that has never been done before. By making yourself marketable by acquiring knowledge, being visible in the industry and maintaining an outstanding personal and professional reputation, you will be setting out on a proven strategy for success.

Questions to ask yourself to help you evaluate your level of marketability include:

- How aware am I of world affairs?
- Am I on top of consumer trends for the year ahead?
- When did I last invest in furthering my industry knowledge?
- Have I acquired any new areas of expertise?
- What steps am I taking to build my professional reputation?
- Is there special event planning recognition that would add value to my portfolio?
- What am I doing to keep myself current and apprised of industry changes?
- What courses have I attended?
- Who am I associating with?
- What books have I read over the course of the past year that will benefit me personally and professionally?

- What magazines do I subscribe to and actually take the time to review?

- What professional organizations do I belong to?

- When did I last research other associations that may hold value?

- What steps am I taking to increase my marketability and earning potential?

2
ACQUIRING AREAS
OF EXPERTISE

Developing areas of expertise is a rewarding investment that you carry forward with you as you move through your life stages and the ranks of your chosen profession. The value of what you have learned never leaves you. Some people make the mistake of spending all their time and energy chained to their desk, hoping that their proven dedication to their job will earn them a promotion or at the very least help them retain their job should there be a downturn. What they don't realize is that by not taking the time to train their mind, acquire new skills and become proficient in new areas, they run the very real risk of not keeping themselves current and marketable should they ever have to seek employment due to layoffs or closures or decide to seek work elsewhere.

The event planning world is an industry that, to the outsider, is steeped in glamour, glitz and power. There are high-powered corporate meetings to attend, executive decisions to be a part of, marketing strategies to create and deliver. It is a field where your imagination and ingenuity are given free realm and you are encouraged not to let your imagination grow stale. Albert Einstein is credited with saying that "Imagination is more important than knowledge."

In the event planning business, developing expertise in both imagination and knowledge are equally important. Corporate clients look to the event planning industry for its expertise in producing innovative ideas, but they also require that their events are planned with military precision and mapped out in great detail. Daily, planners are challenged to find creative ways to meet their clients' event planning objectives, produce guest anticipation, make sure that the dollars they are spending make marketing sense while still allowing them to execute the event logistically and successfully, provide the desire for their client to create another event, and do all this while staying within budget.

You cannot afford to let your mind or your imagination go stale. It can affect you professionally if all you are bringing to the table are recycled ideas and proposals that are churned out using tired concepts. Those in the event planning industry who make sure they create time to invest in themselves, and acquire areas of expertise, find that they have more to offer their employers and clients. By taking the time to pursue knowledge in a variety of ways, they keep themselves current, are on top of trends and come to work with their minds refreshed and full of innovative new ideas. They become multifaceted, and being multitalented they increase their marketability. And the bonus is that some of the most valuable skills in the event planning industry can be acquired while spending quality time with loved ones, family and friends. What could be better for all involved? Acquiring areas of expertise is profitable, personally and professionally.

There are skills that will propel you ahead professionally and give you the competitive edge in business. The key is in knowing which ones will work for you. Many of them are transferable. A top salesperson in the event planning industry began her career straight from selling beverages and had no prior knowledge about the event planning industry. The transferable skill she took with her from one industry to the next was her ability to service, sell and close a deal. She knew that it did not matter what the product was; the same techniques she had learned and been extremely successful with in her past job could be applied to anything. Another sales representative, who had no previous sales skills but was a master of social graces, used that as his jumping-off point. He combined his social skills—knowing how to work a room, make people feel comfortable and network—with that of his industry knowledge, and sold over a million dollars in his first year.

Before you begin to assess your present skills and look at your various options for acquiring new areas of expertise, you first need to decide what your goals in the event planning industry will be. What do you see yourself doing in the next year, in five years and in the long term? If you are looking to acquire areas of expertise that will become your foundation to get you where you envision, and give you a competitive edge in making yourself or your company more marketable, you need to first determine where and what that vision is.

Event planning options today are tremendous. There are so many avenues open to those who wish to pursue a career in this industry. You first need to identify the type of events that you want to be involved in planning and producing. A few choices include those related to:

- The arts (ballet, opera, museums, art exhibits)
- Business (meetings, incentives, conventions, product launches, client appreciation events)
- Entertainment (premieres, award shows, film festivals, gala openings, concerts)
- Fashion (fashion shows, store openings)
- Festivals (wine festivals, art festivals, winter carnivals, film festivals)
- Nonprofit (local, national, charities, political fundraisers)
- Retail (openings, local celebratory events [e.g., parades], fashion shows)
- Social gatherings (informal personal celebrations such as birthdays, anniversaries, bar and bat mitzvahs)
- Society events (gala balls, fundraisers, openings, premieres)
- Sports (local and major sporting events)
- Weddings

Some planners choose to specialize in one field, becoming proficient in that. Others choose diversification so that if one industry hits an economic slump their business will not come to an immediate stop. What *is* of value is learning skills that are interchangeable as you move through doing different styles of events. Developing areas of expertise that will take you further in an event planning career that focuses on doing events for the arts may—or may not—be the same as one centered on working with the business sector. Often there are areas of overlap and the common thread can easily be overlooked. For example, when planning events for the arts, you could very well end up being introduced to and dealing with the same set of corporate executives as you would if you were seeking to handle their business affairs. A number of events for the arts are nonprofit and sponsored by the business community. This could mean dealing with two very different mindsets, and being able to switch gears and relate to both can give you an inside edge. For example, the event for the arts could be a nonprofit fundraiser event that is looking for corporate sponsorship to underwrite the event. The arts committee focus will be on how much publicity the event can generate for its cause and how much money can be raised. The corporate sponsor is looking at what kind of publicity their company will receive, the goodwill that will be generated, the people the event will bring them in contact with and how much the event will cost them. Both sides will be looking at their return on investment. The arts committee is investing its time, energy and contacts, which could help to pull in publicity, while the corporate sponsor is providing its time, resources, money and business credibility to the venture. The event planner handling the art event could very well end up doing spin-off business with the corporate client and handle the company's meetings and social events, as well as planning its personal get-togethers. The planner gets to know the corporate client on a different level, as he hasn't come to the company soliciting business but is introduced to it by the arts committee that opened the door for him. This type of working relationship can be perceived very differently and allows planners to do a soft sell of their services, as opposed to a hard sales call to a corporate buyer. Savvy planners will recognize the opportunity this presents them, maximizing their marketing and business possibilities but doing it with the utmost discretion. The same could very well apply to wedding planning and business. While wedding planners require expertise in diffusing emotional issues, they need to be able speak the language of business as well. Many of the wedding party decision-makers—the bride and groom, their parents and members of the wedding party— are from business backgrounds and want specifics broken out in terms they can relate to and transactions conducted in a businesslike manner.

The movie *Father of the Bride* is a perfect example of a businessman being frustrated with the wedding planner who could not speak his language. The father, who was paying the wedding bill, was equally frustrated by the mounting expenses and unexpected surprises. It is up to the planner to meet clients where they are and talk to them in terms they can understand. Clients do not want to waste their time learning industry lingo or event planning principles. They are hiring professionals so they will *not* have to do that. It has no value to them. They do not want their time eaten up trying to understand the intricacies of what goes into planning an event, taking them away from what is important to them. That is the planner's job.

Those who have mastered the business art of clear communication and who can speak to their clients without weighing them down with jargon and details will stand out from their peers. It is these individuals and firms that will be sought after by clients whether they are planning an artsy affair, a corporate event or a wedding. Business communications has often been an overlooked area of personal development in the event planning industry, but it is one that is worth pursuing as it is completely transferable. While event planning principles remain the same, the clients and the industries you do business with are constantly changing, so being able to easily adapt from one milieu to another will give you and your company a competitive edge.

Once you have identified the types of events, for example, the arts, business, nonprofit, etc., it is important to determine the manner in which you want to do them. For example, some planners may prefer to specialize in small local business events, while others prefer doing large, splashy, corporate, one-of-a-kind, multimillion-dollar extravaganzas around the world. Planners focusing on the nonprofit sector may put their energies into local community fundraising events, while creating gala society fundraisers may be the way to go for another. In both examples, the planners are going after the same market but they are targeting their talents at different ends of the spectrum. In the first case—small local events versus large, splashy corporate events held worldwide—both planners are targeting the business market and sometimes even the same business clients, but for two very different types of events. One planner is choosing to specialize in smaller, low-key events, while the other is soliciting clients' more demanding undertakings. The same applies to the second nonprofit example—two types of events with two very different levels of expertise required, two different nonprofit markets but with the same goal of doing an event to raise funding and/or awareness for a specific cause. One planner is specializing in fundraising events for schools in their district, for example, while another seeks out only high-profile fundraising event projects. Those who long to do high-profile corporate events will not be satisfied if they are limited to doing only small-scale meetings in a local hotel, and not working towards taking on large-scale events or handling a mix of both. Vice versa, some planners excel at meeting the needs of smaller, more complex business meetings and are involved in all aspects, such as audiovisual production, speaker selection and print material development. Knowing your nature and the characteristics of the events you are handling is key. Each style of event comes with its own set of requirements regarding planning skills. It is just as important to know how you want to do events as it is to know which types of events you want to do so that you can develop your expertise to meet this market.

Once you know the type and style of event that you want to do, the next step is deciding which role you are looking at playing in the industry. There are three main roles in event planning:

• Clients

• Event planners

• Suppliers

Clients are the end users. They are the people putting on the event and signing the contracts, and either they or, in the case of fundraisers, their guests will be paying for the event. Event planners design, produce and orchestrate the event for the client. Planners can work for event planning companies, meeting and incentive houses, in-house for corporate clients or independently. In the past, event planners had been the main liaison between the client and the event suppliers. The client signed the main contract with the event planner to manage the event and usually the event planner signed supplier letters of agreement for contracted services on behalf of the client. In some instances, planners, in an attempt to protect themselves from financial repercussions and legal issues, would obtain contracts from the suppliers, have the clients sign the contracts directly without the clients and suppliers ever having met, and just have consulting contracts with their clients for their services. In either case, suppliers worked through the event planners who were deemed to be their clients, and the suppliers' contact with the event planners' customers—who were the end users—was minimal.

Today, lines are blurred and suppliers are competing directly with event planners for clients' business. Their traditional, less visible role of event fulfillment is but a memory. No longer are they just soliciting sales from the event planners and sitting back waiting for an opportunity to bid. They are going directly to the end-user client, knocking on the door and introducing their company and their services. Airlines, hotels (not just the larger chains with national sales offices), transportation companies, destination management companies, decor companies, vendors, venues and restaurants have their own in-house event planning and event management teams that are actively involved in closing sales as a means to building their business, and either are handling the event in partnership with the client and their designated event planning company or cutting out the role of the event planning company completely. Today, no one can afford to sit back and wait for business to walk in, or settle for being one of many bidding on a job without being a part of the qualifying process. Instead, these companies are using their ingenuity to develop new skills that showcase their talents and give them a leg up on their competition.

Event planning as an entity crosses four main business components:

1. Business development

   The business development department is usually comprised of sales and marketing. These two areas may work independently or operate under one umbrella. A company's salespeople are responsible for soliciting sales and servicing their accounts. They initiate sales calls, introduce their company to the client, qualify requests for proposals, brainstorm with the creative design department and contribute ideas for the proposal, lead the sales presentation, manage the account from beginning to end, go on site inspections with the client and are on-site during the actual event.

2. Creative design

   The creative design department is responsible for crafting an event that will meet the client's objectives, impress their guests, stay within budget and provide the client with a positive return on their investment. The department's responsibilities include being ahead of the curve with innovative ideas, research and development, and skilled in event logistics, strategy and negotiation. The division is usually referred to as the planning department. Those involved in the creative process take part in familiarization trips, prepare the client proposal and cost summary, accompany the sales team on client meetings, meet with suppliers, possibly take part in site inspections, secure and review supplier contracts, prepare client contracts and payment schedules and prepare the file for transfer for event management once contracted.

3. Event management

The event management department can also be referred to as operations. Once a program has been sold it moves into operations. Operations is responsible for event orchestration. Under operations, event elements are firmed up, timelines are set, function sheets are prepared, precons (client and supplier review meetings) are set up for a final event walk-through and files are reconciled.

4. On-site production

The on-site production team runs the actual event. The members will be at the site in advance of event move-in, oversee setup, be in charge of the actual event execution, supervise tear-down and move-out, and sign off on final billing.

These four distinct areas are all connected and overlap each other. Each section builds on the next. Layers are added and it is imperative that a solid foundation be in place before moving on to the next stage.

Regardless of whether you work for an event planning company or a supplier, these four main areas will exist in some capacity. In some companies, the role of each staff member is clearly defined. Event planning companies have sales departments, planning or creative departments, operations, and people to handle event execution. Specific people are assigned to handle explicit duties and there is little or no crossover between departments. They all connected but events are handled in an assembly-line process with each person responsible for a certain area. Sales representatives will meet with the client and determine their needs. If a proposal is required, the sales representative will meet with the planning department to lay out the client's requirements. The planning staff prepares the proposal and briefs the sales representative, who in turn presents the proposal to the client. The planning staff may or may not accompany the sales representative to the client meeting. This often depends on the sales rep's personal selling style, management requirements or the client's request. If the proposal is a go, the planning staff requests supplier contracts and prepares for the site inspections, client contract and payment schedule for the sales representative to bring to the client.

Once the contracts are signed, the event is then turned over to the operations department, which will prepare the critical path, work on the program logistics, manage the budget and work with the sales representative and someone from the client's company to finalize details. In many cases the person handling operations is not working directly with the same business contact as the sales representative, but rather someone the client has appointed internally to manage the event. For example, the sales representative may be dealing directly with the company president, CEO, CFO or Vice President of Marketing and Sales, while the event planning staff will be handling day-to-day communication with their key support person, such as an administrative assistant or someone who has been assigned to manage the project and has official decision-making capabilities (e.g., able to authorize changes to the budget). Operations staff may or may not be on-site to orchestrate the actual event. In some cases the file is handed over to program directors who will run the actual event, while in others the operations staff will go on-site. This usually depends on what other events are going on in the event planning office. Sometimes it is not feasible to pull everyone away from other programs they may be working on simultaneously. The sales representative usually is on-site for setup and event orchestration.

In other companies, staff may be required to be involved in all four areas and may be hands on from beginning to end. They may be as actively involved with the key client decision-makers as their company's sales representative. This style of event planning is not necessarily determined by company size or the number of events they do, but sometimes by the event planning company owner's personal style of conducting business. Some use it as a marketing tool, stressing how their events are not passed from hand to hand and that the chances of having something slip through the cracks are lessened from operating their business this way.

Going into event planning, you need to determine which style suits your nature best. For some, for example, Type A personalities who have been defined as having perfectionist tendencies and need to be in control, it can be difficult to plan an event, hand over the file and never get to see firsthand what their minds have conceived. For others, the thrill comes in testing their creativity and helping to land a sale, not in taking on the actual event logistics. They are content to move on to planning the next event without seeing the past one come to fruition, and experience no frustration at not taking the event from beginning to end. You also need to determine whether or not you want to be involved in creating local events, events that will have you revolving around the world non-stop or a mixture of both. Once you have decided what would be your perfect industry fit you can then begin to look at which areas of expertise will further move you personally and professionally along your chosen path, add to your marketability, give you a competitive edge and help you move from one area to another.

1. BUSINESS DEVELOPMENT

Working in business development usually takes you into areas of communication, marketing and sales, and you are generally in a position of meeting with clients face to face. In many cases, the clients' decision-makers are senior executives who will see the event as an expensive venture and want to make sure that they will receive a return on their investment. Of course, this return on investment is not necessarily monetary. An event could be used to foster goodwill in the community or among employees, increase brand recognition, show appreciation to their clients, introduce a new product or motivate sales. It could also be a combination of many things.

Clients are looking to work with people who are up on current events and knowledgeable about their industry. They know you know yours—it is their industry they want you to be focused on. They want you to know who their competition is. In some cases, they even prefer doing business with companies who have done or are doing business with their competition. For example, car companies doing car launches like to work with people who have experience in their particular field. So do direct marketing companies. They know that event planning companies and suppliers hold client confidentiality high and that what you would be proposing for one would not be proposed for the other.

You are dealing with the higher-ups and not all meetings will take place in an office or boardroom. They can be in upscale restaurants or in the client's personal club. Do you have the personal polish to pull that off? Is your knowledge of personal (social) and business etiquette up to standard? For instance, can you discuss wines and do you know what to do when the wine steward goes through the ritual of presenting a bottle of wine for your approval? Is this something that would be personally daunting, or would it be handled with ease as the rest of the table waits for your response? Do you know when the proper time is to order a soufflé? Or when to bring business to the table?

Those choosing to work in business development would do well to invest in books, seminars and personal one-on-one training to acquire expertise in these areas. Books on social etiquette are readily available. *The Etiquette Advantage in Business: Personal Skills for Professional Success* (HarperResource, 1999) by Peggy Post and Peter Post covers everyday manners, and event planning-specific business etiquette can be found in *Event Planning: Ethics & Etiquette: A Principled Approach to the Business of Special Event Management* (John Wiley & Sons, 2003) and the *Do's and Taboos* (John Wiley & Sons) series by Roger E. Axtell. Business etiquette courses and seminars are on the rise. Corporate companies recognize the value and competitive edge of having their executives schooled in these areas and are requiring their staff to be trained in social and business graces. Five-star hotels and top restaurants that cater to the business crowd have identified this need and often conduct private and group seminars on how to order wine, maneuver around the menu, master which fork and spoon to use, handle paying the bill with finesse and other tricks of the trade. Personal instruction can also be requested.

Many top achievers in business development also invest in professional voice coaches and take speaker training so that they are prepared to discuss a variety of subjects and do it with ease. They know that how they present themselves is important and it does not start or stop with their sales presentation. One company owner, who became a leader in her field, hired an image consultant to help her pull together a more professional look. Her preferred manner of dress at the office was comfortable sweats or cozy velour track-style suits and her business wardrobe was extremely casual. She knew she lacked a flair for fashion and turned to an expert in that field for help.

Another colleague—male—made sure that his grooming did not stop with his hair, dress and shoes. He always ensured that his nails were buffed and manicured so that his personal style was not undone by neglecting a very visible area that many top corporate executives pay attention to.

Business can take place on a golf course, tennis or squash court or even a ski slope, and if you have never picked up a golf club before or even hit the bunny (beginner) ski slopes you could be left behind while your peers go out to play business on an executive level. One event planning company's management believes that their employees' aptitude at golf and on the ski slopes has given them an edge on their competition in landing accounts. They took it to the next step and invested in company memberships in a very exclusive golf course, which more than paid for itself. But they did this because they knew that their target market likes to play golf while discussing business, and golf became an essential event element they always included in their meetings, conferences and incentive programs. For some industries, golf is a given. The medical profession, financial industry, car dealerships, insurance companies and pharmaceutical firms are some of the businesses that are known for their love of golf. Sooner or later when you are selling to these markets, especially on an executive level, you will find yourself on a golf course or sitting on the sidelines wishing you were a part of the one-on-one quality time that business golfing affords you. If you know that a potential client has a hot button such as a love for golf, it can pay dividends to play the game and be knowledgeable about it.

If you are focused on being involved in business development, you have to be prepared to meet your clients on their own turf and at their level. Speaking their language is not limited to the language of their industry but extends to what holds personal interest to them. Becoming proficient in business social graces and the games being played will aid in distinguishing yourself and bring you long-term benefit.

2. CREATIVE DESIGN

It is a given that those drawn to creative design will find fulfillment in being able to create imaginative solutions to meet a special need. They will pursue interests that will help to stimulate their creativity and their senses. Being inquisitive and enjoying the task of delving in to research further development of their ideas will be part of their makeup. Being the first to add a new twist to an event element is a challenge they welcome as they strive to push their creativity to the next level. They will be open to acquiring their expertise in new ways, such as by gaining hands-on experience, as it can only help them to become their best.

One planner made a US$100,000 costing error in his proposal because he took the quote the supplier sent at face value. He was not familiar with the special effects that he was proposing and therefore what was written in the supplier's technical rider, which was an addendum to the quote, was meaningless. He had no idea how quickly the expenditures that were required, but not spelled out, would add up. Had he been to a live performance featuring the recommended acts or even taken time to review a tape of a past event, he would have had a multitude of questions. For example, in this case, extensive rigging was required, but no provisions for weights had been factored in, nor had costs for their setup and dismantling, and that was just one tiny aspect. Special flooring was required for the performers. So were dressing rooms, with access to running water and mirrors, for costume changes. The cost of flying in the costumes, as well as having experienced staff on hand to iron and make any necessary repairs, also had to be included. The time to set up the rigging was never questioned, and that reality had a dramatic effect on estimated labor union fees. What this planner needed to do was to familiarize himself with all aspects of this performance so that he could visualize each step of move-in, setup, rehearsals, performance, teardown and move-out. It would have been less costly an error for the company to have flown the employee out to see firsthand what was entailed or to have taken part in—or to have at least visited—a school in their city that was offering courses in the very act he was including in his event.

Someone who has physically been on a golf course, playing or just riding the golf cart, or gone sailing, deep-sea fishing, snorkeling, rock climbing or hot air ballooning, or been to a skateboard, surfing or racing competition, will have a competitive edge over planners who are merely armchair designers. It does not matter that they physically partake of each activity, but that they are active observers. In some cases, event planning companies will pick up the tab for research, while in other cases suppliers are happy to provide planners with a site inspection and run through their particulars in the hopes of being considered for future endeavors—to them it is a welcome sales call they did not have to solicit. Familiarization trips usually offer many opportunities to explore something new. Whether it is a new spa treatment or a chance to try fly-fishing, an opportunity should never be turned down if it affords planners the chance to try or see something new and to witness the participants' responses to the activity. Suppliers, eager to tempt planners to attend their presentations, often do so by including something new, something that hasn't been done before, or by having their events at facilities that will hold planner appeal, ones that they in turn may use or propose to their clients. The more planners learn about a variety of interests, the better their proposals will become. They will be able to speak and plan from firsthand experience. In turn, that will enhance their logistical skills, which planners are able to fine-tune by being able to visualize in minute detail, and enable them to render a more accurate costing to the clients and provide creative options that are tailor-made to fit the client.

Acquiring areas of expertise not limited to creative design will give those in event planning added marketability. Many involved in creating the event are asked to go with their sales representatives, be there through the presentation process and accompany them later on the site inspection. In this capacity, they may be expected to do their part in entertaining members of the executive committee. The same skills that are listed above that are an asset to those in business development—that add value to a sales representative—will be needed by planners.

If planners limit the scope of their learning to just the planning process, which involves only the event design, logistics and negotiations, they will not be as marketable as someone who can converse with the client on an executive level, bring added support to the sales team and help to close a sale.

3. EVENT MANAGEMENT

Once the sale has been contracted and moved into operations, the client's executive committee generally appoints someone from their organization to handle the day-to-day queries their guests may have, and the general questions the event planning operations staff may have. The executives are still involved with the sales representatives regarding event content, final sign-off, budget considerations and any other major areas that require their input and attention, but generally, operations staff does not meet with the company's higher-ups until the pre-event meeting when everyone is gathered together for one final review.

This meeting is the final walk-through before the event commences, and if there are any last-minute changes or additions they are handled at this time. For example, the client may discover at the pre-event meeting that they are coming in under budget due to ongoing negotiations the operations staff have been doing on their behalf, and that they have extra dollars to spend if they choose to do so. In this instance, the operations staff will usually have apprised their sales representative of some viable options that would serve to enhance the event. This meeting, because of its nature and not deliberate scheduling, happens when time is of the essence and everyone is working hard to meet deadlines before the scheduled event. Most of the meetings take place in the client's office and follow a business agenda. Clients may come to the event planning company's offices for rehearsals with speechwriters and a last-minute run through, and lunch or dinner is usually ordered in to save time. Those involved in event operations act as the vital link between what has been contracted and what will be delivered.

This is the time when those in event management have the chance to shine and display their operational and organizational skills and areas of expertise, such as in the instance of being in the enviable position of being able to tell a client that by continuing to work on their behalf to bring in a better program, even after the event has been contracted, they have found ways to save the client money. For the most part, those in event management work behind the scenes, playing a vital but less visible role in an event's success. In some organizations, depending on the workload, the person handling the event may head up on-site operations but still be in the background, or be asked to turn the event over to on-site production.

In event management, being skilled in organization, logistics, timing and budget control are important qualities that event planning companies and their customers look for. Knowledge in customs; protocol; guest safety; time- and cost-saving technology such as online registration; audiovisual, graphic design and printing techniques; and negotiation are all valuable add-on areas of expertise that increase individual and company marketability.

Those in event management can increase their expertise by taking courses, meeting with suppliers during sales calls and attending presentations, but they have an added advantage of being able to learn on the job if they choose to take advantage of what is before them. There are many valuable learning opportunities that many in event management let pass them by, being too intent on finalizing plans to make the time to sit in and be a part of a meeting that will increase their level of expertise. For example, in many cases they are the ones scheduling the production meetings between the client, sales rep and audiovisual house, and do not make the time to sit in on the proceedings. It can only benefit them to do so. They get to learn the language of a different industry; acquire knowledge of how an audiovisual presentation is put together; see firsthand the new technology at work; sample different film techniques; have the opportunity to master sound, lighting and staging from the experts; witness the client's initial reaction; and see the finished product. In the process, they come away knowing more about the client, the client's industry and their specific needs, as well as understanding the audiovisual presentation's logistical components and require- ments, which can only serve to help them deliver a better event and assist them in future negotiations with audiovisual houses. Taking advantage of learning from the experts in fields that impact an event brings added expertise and take-away skills to those involved in event management. The only cost is making time to see what is available—in terms of learning—right in front of you.

4. ON-SITE PRODUCTION

On-site production can be handled by those in event operations or handed over to professional program directors who handle events for a number of planning companies. This is decided by the event planning company owner and senior management, and is based on what else is taking place in the office and the skills that are required on site, such as the ability to speak another language. Pro- fessional program directors run events locally and around the world. The most sought-after program directors are those who bring added value. For example, some program directors speak up to half a dozen languages, which can be a tremendous asset when doing an event out of country or even one locally where translation is needed for invited guests. International guests like to be able to converse with someone in their own language. It makes them feel cared for and the client gains extra points for thoughtfulness. The program directors that are most in demand are also skilled in diplo- macy, protocol and social graces. While in-house event planning staff may be limited as to the number of events they can be out of the office to handle, some professional program directors work 365 days a year traveling from one event to another. Due to the sheer volume of events they have managed, they have likely encountered every situation imaginable, learned crisis management techniques from many of the top event planning companies and know how to handle most situations with finesse. They spend time learning about the country they may be traveling to—customs, protocol, sightseeing locations and shopping areas—as well as the guest group's demographics, and are usually fully prepared to handle questions from a guest's perspective. They are often skilled negotiators and work to reduce costs even further on-site where they can, having become adept at identifying areas of savings from working with so many different suppliers and vendors around the world. They bring their years of on-site experience and expertise with them to each event that they do.

Some event planning companies pay a premium and contract their program directors exclusively. They know that having certain individuals available to clients adds to their marketability and gives them a competitive edge. And program directors that bring this added value often have more work than they can handle. Learning the skills that are requested most in program directors—diplomacy, protocol, social graces, crisis management, negotiation and the ability to speak different languages—can only benefit the career of someone that is in event management and greater enhance the marketability of those in creative design and business development.

ACQUIRING EXPERTISE

There are several methods to acquire areas of expertise and they don't have to be all work and no play, be major time or financial investments, or necessarily done on your own or only with business colleagues. There are four main ways of acquiring experience:

- On-the-Job Training
- Industry Resources
- Targeted Professional Evolvement
- Pursuit of Personal Passions

ON-THE-JOB TRAINING

On-the-job training is sometimes done on the fly. You step into the event planning whirlwind of deadlines and there never seems to be enough time to set aside to share knowledge. Bad habits can go unchecked, and be passed on to newcomers, and the vicious cycle becomes never-ending. A company that wants to give itself the competitive edge makes sure that there is time allotted for training and even schedules it to take place out of the office to avoid interruptions. It wants its employees to know the company's mission statement, what the company stands for and how it expects its representatives to act on its behalf. Standards to be met are made clear and policy and procedures are outlined in a company manual that those new on the job can refer to. Company etiquette, the standards of ethics and the codes of behavior are known by all. The office acts as a well-oiled machine because it has proper maintenance. For example, a company standard may be that even quick e-mails going out to a supplier must be as professionally phrased in business language as they would be if going to a client and must contain no personal or company information that would be considered unprofessional. That means without the adornment of smiley faces or computer terms such as LOL being used, which is sometimes used in casual e-mail communication between close family members and friends. Newspapers covering scandal-making corporations often back up their quotes referring to e-mails long forgotten by the actual sender. When you send an e-mail or letter out, you never know who will be reading it. E-mails are easily saved and just as easily forwarded on to others you may have no intention or no knowledge of sharing information with. Company training in etiquette, standards and behavior will ground you in the basics.

Some event planning firms hold weekly meetings, bringing everyone together for a quick update. While this can pull you away from pressing deadlines, if the time is set and consistent then you can plan for it, and such meetings could prove to be time well spent if managed properly. You never know who, thanks to experience, may have the solution to a vexing problem. One planner was struggling with how to handle the special requirements for a circus act that was taking place as part of a product launch, and the answer literally turned out to be sitting right beside her. Someone else on the team had worked on the same type of show and supplied the solution. You do not always know what the person next to you knows. Your neighbor could be the perfect resource for you. Meetings enable everyone to share what they have worked on, thereby offering ideas and solutions.

Event planning companies that want to learn from the good as well as the bad also make time to schedule event reviews back in the office. They conduct an in-depth review of the event from all perspectives—client, business development, creative design, event management, on-site production, suppliers—to determine what worked, what they learned, what they would do next time if certain situations arose, and whether or not the event met their client's objectives. Some companies treat this so seriously that they bring in temporary staff to answer the telephones so that everyone can take part in the discussion and learn from one another. From each event, you will come away with something that you would do differently given another chance, and you will have learned other tricks of the trade from watching how your suppliers conduct their business. The goal of having an event review is to take the best to your next event and learn what not to do again from the rest.

Industry Resources

The event planning industry provides a wealth of information, training options and learning options from a variety of sources. The opportunities to acquire new areas of expertise, learn from those who have mastered their craft and increase your level of knowledge in your chosen field are endless. Some require only your time, others you can participate in for minimal personal cost, while certain others, such as industry magazines, newspaper subscriptions and familiarization trips, are supplied by event planning companies as part of their business expenses. Some industry resources available include:

- Supplier Sales Representatives
- Industry Presentations
- Familiarization Trips
- Associations
- Industry Publications
- Industry Trade Shows
- Industry Award Shows

Supplier Sales Representatives

Supplier sales representatives are a resource just waiting to be tapped and can provide planners with inside information that you will not find simply reading the brochure. The key is being selective with suppliers you choose to spend time with and do business with. There isn't enough time in the day for meetings with every supplier that would love to tell you about their products in sometimes seemingly exhaustive detail if they are merely coming into your office reciting their brochure by rote. That holds no value to you or to them in the end. Who you want coming through your door are suppliers whose product matches your clientele's needs. If your clients want to stay in only five- and six-star resorts, spending time with a representative who markets three- and four-star properties is not productive. Of course, the reverse is true if your clients would not dream of staying in a luxury property as that is not the image they want to project. That doesn't mean that you won't someday have a client for whom the suppliers' products might be the perfect fit, but your time is better spent with suppliers who meet your needs today. If you want to acquire areas of expertise, you have to start with prioritizing your day and limit your time to what will move you and your company ahead. You can still be gracious to the company that you are not inviting in to meet personally with you. Have them send in their material and business card to keep on file but limit your exposure at this time. You cannot afford to waste time you don't have in an effort to be nice; don't forget that you would also be wasting the time of the sales rep in the process.

Be very specific about your needs when setting up supplier meetings. Let them know what you want to achieve in the time spent together and what you expect to have learned at the end of it. Some hotel representatives have never been to the properties they are representing and unless they have done their homework, they may not be able to share with you anything that you can't find out from the brochure. Other reps, although they may not have been to a property, can tell you about every nook and cranny. They can even recommend where and why a group breakfast should be served in a particular setting. Those are the details that you want to know as a planner. The brochure may not tell you that if you hold your cocktail reception on a certain terrace situated on a certain cliff, the guests will see the most spectacular sunset over the ocean with surfers still visible below. Add a classical guitarist in the background and you have set the scene for a memorable event moment. And the well-prepared sales rep can tell you exactly which classical guitarist has been winning rave reviews and they will have a CD to leave with you. In the planner's mind, they will have planted a very powerful seed.

One planner was so excited to learn about a new property that he felt would be the perfect fit for one of his clients that he called them up on the spot to tell them about it. The result of that call was three back-to-back events that took place within two months of the salesperson making the sales call. The result was a half-million dollars worth of unexpected business. The sales rep excited the planner, who in turn was able to impart that excitement to his client and make an unexpected sale in the process. And this venue was not inexpensive. The planner did not let a tight economy hold him back from presenting something he knew would have great appeal to his client. The event planning company enhanced its value to the client by bringing something that proved to be of great benefit.

 Learn from the pros. Spend time with sales representatives who display a true understanding of what it takes to meet your needs, get you excited and teach you ways to help you to sell their product to your client. Listen to their sales techniques and benefit from their sales expertise.

Industry Presentations

Industry presentations are an excellent place to learn what to do and what not to do. You often get to experience new venues, and you may witness some interesting mishaps. Each one teaches you something. One exciting new venue made the news but not necessarily in the way it hoped. The main room featured an exquisite fountain that would have benefited from extra lighting. One of their guests made quite a splash when she accidentally stepped into the fountain and drenched her shoes. Attending event planners were sure to remember that in future they would ensure that guests are protected from getting soaked in this or any other venue with a fountain.

Being an attendee allows planners to experience things from a guest perspective and that can be of tremendous value. With each event you attend, you will come away with a mental checklist of new considerations to be aware of when planning your next event. If the only events you ever attend are the ones you plan, you will lose out on a great learning opportunity. It is not essential to go to every event to which you are invited, but if an invitation comes in that has the potential to introduce you to something new—in whatever form—give attending serious consideration. One planner, impressed by the way staff at the opening of a new entertainment complex had their act together, booked the venue to host an event that would take place within weeks of its opening. Normally, planners give a new venue six months to get up and running and work out the kinks before holding an event there. Seeing firsthand how smooth the operations were at the venue's opening and how the experienced staff easily handled over 2,000 guests gave the planner confidence to move ahead more quickly than they traditionally might have and try something that had never been done before. The client was impressed, the guests were wowed and the planner's reputation for doing spectacular events grew.

> **T**
> **I**
> **P**
> At presentations, make it a point to sit beside someone new whenever you can. If the presentation includes a sit-down dinner with open seating, look for empty seats at tables where the suppliers or their representatives are seated. You may be able to pick up valuable information about their property or services in casual conversation that others attending the event will not be privy to.

Familiarization Trips

Familiarization trips can take place anywhere in the world and can be hosted by an airline, tourist board, hotel, venue, restaurant, destination management company or a combination of them. Suppliers personally select and invite event planning companies to come and experience what they have to offer. While familiarization trips are used as marketing and educational tools, suppliers are looking for a return on their investment and seek active participation by those event planning companies that are likely to do business with them. A familiarization trip could be something a planner does on his own, for example, stay overnight at a local resort to sample its services, or as part of a larger group. Attendees could be from across the country or from the same neighborhood. Conceivably, planners could find themselves taking part in a familiarization trip with their most fierce competition, who will also be paying special attention to what is being said.

Familiarization trips are a great opportunity to play—not around or with your reputation but to partake in new activities. The more you can experience firsthand, the more expertise you will acquire. If you are offered, for example, the opportunity to fly over Las Vegas at night in a helicopter, rollerblade on Venice Beach, try snorkeling in renowned reefs, go hot air ballooning at sunrise in Arizona or horseback riding in Hawaii, or learn about fine wines in Napa, take it. Given the chance to do something that they would include in an event or that would teach them something new that they could add to their portfolio, some planners choose instead to go shopping, lie by the pool or have a few drinks during their leisure time. Others, intent on acquiring new areas of expertise, take advantage of what is put before them and research other options to explore, time permitting. They set out with a list in hand, not wasting a moment of free time. If your competition is there, getting involved, seeking out new ideas, you cannot afford to be left behind. Of course, your plan may be to spend time getting to know your supplier or members of their team better; admittedly, having one-on-one time to talk can be valuable as well. In a group situation, with your competitors around you, certain areas of discussion are just not feasible. For example, you will not be open to talking about which property or type of activity a certain client may be receptive to, as you do not want to give the competition you know, and those you may not be aware of, any insider company information that may benefit them in their next proposal.

> **T**
> **I**
> **P**
>
> Take stock of where, when and how you can build up your level of expertise, such as taking part in a new activity even if it is only in the capacity of an observer. For example, don't miss out on a chance to see how white-water rafting is done, even though you may not be comfortable actually taking part in it for personal reasons (e.g., inability to swim, tendency for motion sickness, etc.). Go to see the setup, watch from the shore and make transportation arrangements to meet the group where it disembarks. Doing that will enable a planner to see how an operation is run and what to put in place for guests when they plan such an event. Having acquired the knowledge in order to be able to discuss various situations with clients at the planning stages allows planners to include creative options in their proposals that others may not have thought of, as well as enabling them to capture any necessary costs that may not be spelled out in supplier quotes.

Associations

Associations are an excellent source of knowledge, networking and inspiration. Along with monthly meetings and educational seminars, many associations also put on annual national and world conferences. Many of them produce monthly publications such as magazines and newsletters. To benefit from the best associations have to offer and to aid in the quest of acquiring personal marketable areas of expertise, get actively involved. Attending a meeting here or there will not give you full value. Some suppliers and planners increase their knowledge by volunteering to help organize educational conferences. They make sure that they serve on committees with people they want to learn from, and build relationships with these industry mentors. The skills they take away help them carve out their own successful career. They deliberately get involved in areas that offer them a learning experience and in turn share their expertise with others. One planner worked on perfecting her presentation skills by volunteering with an association, first to do meeting announcements and speaker introductions, then facilitate meetings and finally speak at association events. She felt comfortable speaking in front of people she knew and that in turn helped to prepare her for speaking in front of clients and doing announcements on-site, such as imparting instructions to guests regarding event arrangements at the end of a meeting or group function. When she started out, she was terrified of speaking in front of participants and shied away even from doing a simple announcement on a motorcoach. She knew her fears were limiting her from moving ahead, and felt that by getting involved with the association, she could learn from those who had mastered public speaking and do it in a safe place, among her peers.

T
I
P

Direct your energies into the areas that matter most to you. Focus on what will bring you expertise in the sectors you want to grow in. Don't be afraid to pass up getting involved in what will only serve to be a time distraction for you—not necessarily someone else—and prevent you from achieving your specific goals. For example, don't accept a position on the board as treasurer if what you are seeking is an opportunity to not only be involved, but be involved in a way will also provide you with opportunities to enhance your public-speaking abilities. Your needs may be better met working on the education or communication committee where you can learn from experts in those fields, while the treasurer position may be better filled by someone who is eager to learn more about business accounting. Make sure that you do not misuse your time or let a learning opportunity pass you by.

Industry Publications

Industry publications afford you a quick read on what is currently taking place in event planning. A list of some of the top industry print and online publications can be found in Appendix C. Industry publications will keep you apprised of hot topics, coming trends, new products, book reviews and tips and techniques that have proven to be successful in the past. Leaders in the event planning industry are often used as story sources, giving their perspective and contributing to articles by sharing their expertise. Industry publications also keep you informed of moves and promotions in the industry, job opportunities, and which company is handling which client for what type of event, all of which has added value. Making the time to read the magazines or newsletters is an easy way to keep your finger on the pulse of the industry. In busy times you may not be able to do more than quickly skim publications that arrive on your desk but mark the articles that hold interest so that you can return to them later for a more lengthy read during a commute to work, on a break or during an evening designated to catching up on industry news. Make a note of any relevant website addresses and contact information as you read and enter them immediately into your card file or address book. You can waste time trying to go back through stacks of magazines trying to re-find important information that was not catalogued as you came across it. Many magazines include forms to order information on suppliers appearing in the current issue, and it is a good practice to fill these in and send them back so that you can do further research on products and venues that have piqued your interest.

Along with industry publications, consumer lifestyle, food and design magazines are also a good source of inspiration and keep planners apprised of past, current and coming trends.

Industry Trade Shows

Industry trade shows are a great opportunity to scout out new products and see new marketing ploys firsthand, as well as to network with suppliers and colleagues. They can also provide creative ideas for future events. Take the time to note the displays that have been set up and what attracts you to them. Many times, suppliers showcase innovative themes to capture a planner's imagination and draw people in. They know that market research has shown that they have only about 20 seconds to grab your attention, and generally they take great care with finding a marketing hook. For example, one resort known for its superb golf courses set up a putting green and brought in a well-known golf pro who was associated with its courses to offer tips and techniques to those who dropped by its booth. Another hotel, known for its spa, yoga and Pilates, enticed male clients by having top jocks talk about how they use yoga and Pilates to give them a competitive edge in their sports. Suppliers know that done successfully, this gives them an edge on their competition, as the more time that they can keep you captive or at least captivated, the less time you can spend with their competition. They will pull out all the stops to achieve their goal. This is the suppliers' time to shine, and if their display and attitude is lackluster at such a critical time, maybe their products and services are as well. But even negative encounters can be a learning experience. If you can define what turned you off and held no appeal, you can ensure that it is never a part of your company's repertoire when presenting to clients.

> When attending trade shows, try not to be weighed down by too many brochures. Many suppliers will ship the brochures to your office for you and some trade shows provide on-site complimentary shipping services—make sure that you avail yourself of these offers. If you are burdened with heavy bags, it will have a negative effect on your mood, energy level and focus.

Industry Award Shows

The event planning industry honors its own at industry award shows, many of which are listed in Appendix D. Companies up for nomination know the added value an award can bring to their business. The added prestige enhances their business and professional reputation and attracts new clients. Who doesn't want to be associated with some of the best designed events in the industry? Some event planning companies make it their priority to pursue industry awards and nominations—the industry's stamp of approval on having done outstanding work. Client approval is usually obtained before submitting entries for nomination, because clients may be reluctant to have their event in the limelight. Others look on it as an opportunity to shine in their own industry. Being part of an award-winning group can help the client attract top employees to the firm and bring positive attention to their company. If its event wins an award, it and the winning event planning company can use that as a marketing vehicle and a reason to communicate with customers.

Attending award shows gives planners the chance to see what others have done. They may have customers in the same industry and it is always good to be on top of what their customer's competition has done. They can also come away with new ideas to incorporate—not copy—into their own designs. No one wants to produce cookie-cutter events. Top planners may see an idea and then look for ways to make it their own, giving it a new twist or taking it to a new level. For example, in California, live actors dressed in costume have been taking part in a masters living arts festival for years. They are made up to look like replica paintings and literally step into the picture frame and hold the pose. Floral arrangers seeing this technique put their spin on it and created living framed floral arrangements. Sometimes, all planners need to see is something that takes hold of their imagination and they are off and running with a completely new theme idea, one that bears no resemblance to the one that twigged their imagination. What they have been presented with is a new way of looking at something that may have been overused and should now be retired. For example, serving traditional hot chocolate at an après-ski event became passé. Serving white hot chocolate became something new. Specialty coffees and hot chocolates then became all the rage. The movie *Chocolat* would have inspired a more spicy hot chocolate creation being served at events. Surprising guests with New York's famous Serendipity 3's Frrrozen Hot Chocolate (which can now be purchased and shipped from www.serendipity3.com) instead of the expected traditional or white hot chocolate would offer guests a frosty, unexpected taste treat and not something they could find at their local coffee shop. Serving traditional hot chocolate would lack an imaginative flair unless the theme menu is reflective of featuring comfort foods or a nostalgic 1950s or 1960s ski party.

When colleagues are being awarded the industry's top honors, whoever is hosting the show is sure to make every effort to impress. This includes the venue, the florist, the decor company and the evening's entertainment. This is their opportunity to showcase their talents as well and to create an event that will rival the award winners in special touches. Not only can you end up being dazzled by award nominees' designs, you can also come away delighted with the new knowledge you have picked up by attending the award show. There is generally a cost to attend award presentation shows, but the expenditure is usually well worth it to further your education and have the opportunity to meet some of the industry's top performers.

If you can't attend the award show in person, make sure that you follow the results reported in the industry newspapers and magazines so that you are on top of winning event designs and the suppliers who helped to produce the outstanding results. Always embrace the opportunities that are presented to you to learn from those who are masters of their craft. Staying on top of *their* game, not just yours, can help to give you a competitive edge as well.

 Some award shows provide opportunities to volunteer your time or offer your company's services. This can be an excellent marketing opportunity to present yourself or your business to a very targeted and talented audience.

TARGETED PROFESSIONAL EVOLVEMENT

Once you have determined the area that you wish to focus your personal and professional business growth in, whether it is business development, creative design, event management or on-site production, you can begin to map out your strategy for success by acquiring areas of expertise that are geared to the direction you want to move in.

One up-and-coming sales representative was determined never to be left behind if an opportunity to play golf with her clients came up. She knew that golf was her clients' passion. She realized that she only had so much time in the day to exercise, and that while her personal preference was to go to the gym, she knew that it would not help her to evolve in her job and grow to the next level. She decided to forgo the gym. Mastering the treadmill did not offer the same growth potential as mastering a golf club would. She decided to make learning golf a priority and was up every morning at 6:00 a.m., practicing on the public golf course near her home before going in to work, walking the course for added exercise. The money she would have spent in a fitness club membership was invested instead in learning the business game of golf. She signed up for golf clinics and one-on-one instruction.

When she traveled for work, she took advantage of being able to play on some of the best courses in the world and to learn from top pros. An added benefit of being out on the golf course was that she was able to pick up new ideas that she could use in the office and propose to those of her clients planning to include golf tournaments as part of their events. She discovered new features to enhance golf tournaments, including mobile barbecues rather than traditional sandwich carts or box lunches. She learned she could add ice cream machines, specialty coffee and other themed beverage bars at various holes. She learned she could photograph participants' golf swings to be analyzed by the resident pro. By listening to golfers, she also learned trends and venues that were becoming passé and which courses were every golfer's dream—such as the one U.S. course that stretched across a border and was being promoted as having the only international golf hole in the world and an extra-long private runway so company executives could arrive by jet. When one of her clients was looking for the ultimate golf getaway for an executive retreat, she knew exactly how to target her proposal and which location would hold the most appeal. By mastering a sport that had business value in many areas, she was able to give herself a competitive edge. Had she continued to invest her time and energy in her health club, she would have strengthened her muscles but not her options.

Alternatively, belonging to an exclusive health club could give other planners a business advantage. You have to know exactly who you are marketing yourself and your talents to. One individual who represented exclusive locations for both the event planning and film industry became a member at the health club of one of his city's most upscale hotels. He was not concerned that it was a 30-minute commute from his home and office. When film executives and stars came to town, this was the hotel that was most favored. Because it is the nature of film industry people to work out, he knew that he was putting himself in a target-rich environment. Because he was adept in weight lifting, he stood out from other hotel guests and was often engaged in conversational chitchat about his techniques. Relaxing in the hot tub or in the sauna after a workout enabled him to meet people he might not have had the opportunity to otherwise. For him, investing in fitness and joining a club where it could advance his career had great value and it paid off in business and referrals. He also joined a well-respected nonprofit organization that was supported by the film industry. It put on special screenings where top directors flew in to discuss their work. Again, this gave him an opportunity to mix and mingle with potential clients, and in the process he became very knowledgeable about their industry and was able to further advance his talents.

An aspiring program director, short on funds but long on spare time during her commute, used her time to study different languages through books on tape, which she obtained with a minimal library rental fee. Becoming accomplished in many other languages allowed her to increase her marketability and moved her ahead in her field. She did not make acquiring knowledge and expertise about money or time. She found a creative way to learn that more than paid for itself.

One very successful event planning company owner insists that the first thing her staff does is familiarize themselves with the morning's top financial newspapers. Everyone from the receptionist to senior management scans the papers for information on their clients and their clients' competition. They discuss these current events and use the information from the newspapers to establish a connection, and send out letters of congratulation to their customers and potential clients on successful ventures and promotions. The event planning company knows that being on top of current events and being able to converse shrewdly on a number of subjects that are relevant to them is a priority to its clients. It has been effective in attracting major corporations to the event planning company. The staff presents a group image of being cultured, refined, well-read and well-spoken and these are the qualities that have value to their clients. The planners make sure they are reading what their clients read and that is what sets them apart from their competition. Their clients are steeped in business and want to work with a company that understands their world and can speak the language of their industry. Doing so makes the event planning company easier to relate to and it has served to increase its marketability.

One event planner even got paid while she learned to perfect her craft. Her love was tabletop decor and although she was very artistic, she did not have expertise in the care and handling of floral arrangements. She took a part-time job as a florist's assistant to learn more about the care of flowers. As her skills grew, she started to create her own designs at home and turned the expertise she gained working in a florist shop into a million-dollar business.

PURSUIT OF PERSONAL PASSIONS

Going to the movies, attending the theater, playing tennis, sailing, bowling, playing pool and visiting one-of-a-kind shows are simple, everyday passions that will help you take away new knowledge to advance your career. There are literally thousands of such activities, but it is selecting the right ones that makes the difference. Learning how to sail may not be an indulgence if your clients love to take part in sailing regattas. Even watching television has value and can sharpen your creative skills. To those working in event planning, a multitude of ideas can be picked up from watching shows like *Survivor* and *The Amazing Race*. Some of their team challenges can provide inspiration that could be used at corporate team-building events. Movies filled with special effects (a laser sequence can become the basis of a laser obstacle course for a high-tech client looking for a fun icebreaker), or live shows like Cirque du Soleil or by master magicians can leave creative minds spinning as they exit the theater. Anyone in the industry experiencing David Copperfield creating a snowstorm in a theater would be on the telephone the next day finding out how to do it and looking to see how they could include either the snowstorm trick or Copperfield himself in a winter fantasy theme.

It is critical to know which areas of expertise to target and choose the ones that will put you ahead of the curve. This will help you and your company to stretch and evolve. The stakes are high. What you are selling and marketing is not just a product but a total package. Clients are spending their time and their money doing business with those with whom they have a business, intellectual and emotional connection. Companies don't want to do business with talking heads who say only what they think the client wants to hear. They prefer to work closely and develop business relationships with individuals and companies they believe truly know and understand what they do, are aware of their business needs and future objectives and can offer them intelligent insight and innovative solutions. They value those who can speak their language and who know instinctively how they like to conduct business as a company. Developing expertise in areas that have client appeal in your chosen field, along with developing exceptional event planning skills, will increase the marketability of companies and individuals and set them apart from their competition. Your skills and abilities become part of your personal or company persona—your essence. They add layers of nuances of marketability that may be indescribable in a proposal but comes across in person, which can be the key to landing an account, your dream job or a promotion.

Acquiring areas of expertise becomes a strong foundation to build on and is valuable personally and professionally. From the personal side, continuing your pursuit of knowledge—and this does not mean just academically—helps you lead a life that is not one-dimensional.

Questions to help determine which areas of expertise would be most beneficial to you include:

- What type of events do I want to do?
- What role do I want to play in the industry?
- What area do I want to work in?
- What knowledge and skills do I already possess that will be an asset?
- What areas of expertise do I need to develop that will increase my marketability?
- What on-the-job learning opportunities can I take advantage of?
- What industry resources do I need to research?
- What common interests do my clients share?
- What are my personal passions?
- Where do I need to focus my energies first?
- What are three critical things I can do to start gaining expertise in each of the areas I want to grow in?

3
CREATING YOUR NICHE

Event planning companies and their suppliers work ceaselessly to present their clients with creative options that will meet their objectives and give them a return on their investment. What many in the event planning industry neglect to do is apply that same philosophy to themselves and their business. Many companies focus on closing the next sale, executing an upcoming event and wrapping up one that has just taken place, never stopping to look at whether or not they themselves are profiting.

A return on investment can encompass many things. It is not always tied to immediate financial gain. Some companies take on events for little or no money, doing them instead for the prestige and the ability to say that they were associated with it, and to be able to add the event to their client list. For them, the return on investment is to enhance their reputation, not their bank account. Others take on demanding clients that the rest of the industry is tiptoeing around because they know that handling their business will allow them to develop new areas of expertise. And the short-term emotional cost of doing business with them is worth the return of hands-on knowledge.

Why would they willingly put themselves through this? Companies and individuals who have defined the area they wish to work in are doing whatever it takes to make it their niche and to become known. Instead of chasing the same companies as everyone else, their focus is creating a niche market where they can stand out. They target their products and skills to cater to very distinct markets and to where they may be one of the few companies catering to a specific clientele.

Events come in all sizes with different requirements and a sliding scale of budgets. For example, a meeting to one company may be 50 sales representatives holding a meeting in a local venue, with coffee and tea served and very little else. For another company, a meeting may mean bringing together hundreds if not thousands of their company employees for a meeting that has guest speakers flown in, a major audiovisual presentation, extensive food and beverage, and transportation requirements. And niche markets can be created to service both large and small groups.

One corporation used to annually charter several private aircraft at a time to fly its staff in from across the country, and do a huge three-day blowout that ran in the millions of dollars. Event planning companies' sales reps, anxious to land major accounts, would focus their energy and their office's on trying to win this business away from the incumbent, with little success. A great deal of time and money was lost on trying to obtain an account they may not have been fully equipped to handle had they won it. In actuality, the profit was not as great as the sales reps imagined it would be. In addition, the amount of time servicing this one account left little time to take on other new accounts so they could grow their business. The event planning company that was handling this account put itself in the precarious position of all its income walking out of the door if its client ever left it—and they eventually did—with nothing in place to withstand the financial loss.

In the meantime, companies holding smaller meetings with conceivably less dollars to spend were languishing from the lack of sales rep attention. They failed to realize that the markups may be better on smaller accounts, that there were ways to increase their income, and that their company may have more stability if it was based on having a number of accounts in different industries as opposed to just one major demanding account that could leave any time. This applies not only to meetings but all types of events. For example, many planners would love to design high-profile events for Fashion Week in New York, but fashion shows go on continually and require event planning expertise across many malls in America and in large upscale retail stores. Gaining expertise and becoming known in the fashion arena could one day lead to doing events for the larger fashion houses.

Sales reps chase the large car launch accounts but seldom call on individual dealerships to work with them on their events and promotional campaigns, which could lead to their being recommended to handle larger events. An example of a niche market in the automobile industry is a company set up to transport and detail the cars that are on display at automotive consumer trade shows, media events and product launches. How the cars look inside and out, how they are displayed (e.g., with custom hubcaps positioned so that the company logo is exactly where it is meant to be), and having someone to care for and refresh the cars (e.g., remove marks, fingerprints, etc.) between shows are important event elements for car manufacturers. So is working with a company that excels at moving, off-loading, setting up and tearing down car displays and has expertise in working with fire marshals in meeting and enforcing fire, insurance and permits regulations and building codes.

Some planners have recognized that their desires, talents and expertise lend themselves to creating a niche market, where they strive to become an event planning company *sui generis*—a sought-after event planning company that can offer its clients something unique and in doing so become a category of its own. Instead of chasing the same business as their peers, some planners are busy creating their own market that will put them in demand and have clients calling them.

Niche markets come in all sizes. Some event planning companies specialize in niche markets that cater to smaller group numbers, while others target their talents and make their mark handling niche market events that are done on a large scale. You can create a niche that is:

- Meeting a Need
- A Specialty Market
- Income Driven
- An Emotional Hot Button
- Specialized Expertise

MEETING A NEED

Companies and individuals looking to create their niche in the event planning field research their available options within specific event planning categories such as:

- Corporate events
- Social events
- Community events
- Nonprofit events

They look to see who the majority are targeting and determine if there is an area that is not being serviced for whatever reason. For example, you may decide that you want to do only corporate events. But under the umbrella of corporate events, there are many factors to consider. Do you want to do events for large or small businesses? Are you prepared to do events around the world or is your preference local or national functions? Will you take on a company's meetings and conferences or do you want to do only their special events and incentive programs? Planning meetings and conferences can appear to be routine, so would you rather do something that will allow you to be more creative? Are you prepared to handle the logistics of an event for 2,000 or does the very thought of it make you feel weak at the knees? Is your expertise in the financial arena or in doing intricate product launches? What special skills do you or your company have that would be of great value to a specific type of client? Could you handle servicing a company that requires constant handholding and having you available 24/7, or do you need to work with businesses that are clear minded in their requirements and are only looking to you to fulfill them?

One event planning company owner decided to take a step back and look at where her competition was focusing their energies. She found that the major players were going after the same bit of business. Each company involved in the bidding frenzy was spending valuable time, money and resources trying to land the same accounts, but in the end only one would come out a winner. It just didn't make good business sense. The clients that she found everyone was focused on all had big budgets and did international travel. No one was targeting small businesses with perceived limited funds that were looking to do meetings closer to home and without big budget fanfare such as theme decor and entertainment. These small companies, she discovered, suited her skills and her lifestyle best. She decide to make this overlooked market her niche. Her reputation and her business grew and her decision turned out to be very profitable. While she may not have been doing theme parties any longer, many of her clients were using very sophisticated audiovisual setups, bringing in name speakers, arranging for staff training and asking her to help them produce promotional material for their meetings. In the end, many of the budgets turned out to be equal to those of companies doing meetings that contained more splashy event elements; they just spent their money differently. Her company became indispensable to her clients and in the time when air travel came to a halt her business was not affected.

Another event planning company created its niche by concentrating on events that are high profile, big budget and needed to be filled with celebrities. Planners knew their clients wanted the media to be buzzing about the events they threw and they knew that they had the creativity, the expertise and the contacts to pull it off. They were schooled in public relations and knew how to work with the media to gain maximum exposure. Their clients depended on them for all of their special events large or small around the world not only because of what they knew how to do but also *who* they knew. They mastered the art of being able to create events that attract media interest, having them vying to attend their clients' events and splash their parties across the news. With each event they did, their marketability soared and attracted new clients who were looking for someone to produce the same type of events and publicity for them. How did they achieve this?

The event planning company owner amassed one of the most sought-after guest lists and the only way to access it was to hire him. As part of his services, he would arrange to invite some very special guests to attend his clients' events. The names on his list were the ones listed in boldface in most newspapers and only he, not his clients, had access to their contact information. He collected his roster of names by volunteering to head up various committees for gala fundraisers. He made sure to be a part of fundraising endeavors that would bring him in close contact with people he needed to know. As telephone lists are usually compiled and very closely guarded he made sure—in exchange for his time—that he managed to be involved at a level that would gain him access to both the list and the people he wished to network and develop business friendships with.

He had also developed an innate ability to match the right guests to the right event and always ensured that they were VIP'd by his clients. He matched a corporate need with his niche and was very successful. He knew that many high-society events pay top celebrities in one form or another to attend. There is added promotional value to the client in having well-known names being photographed at their event, showing visible endorsement of their product or cause, and that was what he was able to provide for his clients. Gala fundraisers have long known the marketability of having top-name entertainers to perform at their events. Fundraisers understand that they need a name that will pull people in if they are looking to raise millions of dollars and charge thousands of dollars a couple to attend their event, and they are willing to pay an entertainment fee to have the right name to help them sell tickets.

SPECIALTY MARKET

Specialty markets can sometimes be described as the tucked away and overlooked little markets that grew into something bigger than anyone would have imagined. The world of retail provides excellent examples to learn from. Specialty stores, magazines and travel are everywhere you turn these days. Companies catering to very specific needs are growing, while those who try to offer something for everyone are folding—they haven't defined their market or they are busy trying to continually revamp their image instead of reinventing what they are selling and focusing on what the consumer is buying.

For example, some clothing stores make selling to the very tall their specialty niche, while others seek out customers who are very petite. These stores are addressing a consumer need and offer a very different selection that draws customers to them. Major department stores trying to offer clothing for children, teens, ladies, men or specialty sizes sometimes miss the mark, and many such companies that once seemed invincible have closed their doors. Health food stores have created their niche, as have fantasy candy emporiums. One candy store in New York carries thousands of types of candies from all over the world. It markets itself as the ultimate candy store in the world and has been so successful that it is opening several new locations in the U.S. It is expanding despite the national fitness obsession. It has tapped into and made candy its niche. If you are going to splurge on candy, why not do it right and make it a memorable experience in the process? Staff cater to customers in the store and online and have expanded to doing parties and in-store events.

One candy store has a party room that can be rented for special occasions. Entertainment can be brought in and both large and small groups can be managed. People of all ages—the very young and the young at heart—can enjoy creating chocolate sculptures that can be decorated with edible paints (that can also be purchased for use in more adult painting pursuits at a later time), and making chocolate lollipops, candy picture frames and candy jewelry. These are all options on its party menu. While it sells to the public, many of its items would be perfect for event planning theme party additions. It has old-time favorites that would be perfect for parties based on the 1950s, 1960s and 1970s, and even edible topiaries that can be used as centerpieces, buffet decor or an interesting corporate gift to be shared by staff. It has its niche covered on all ends. By tapping into many markets with one product, it is not limiting its growth or its revenue source.

One fast-food company saw a specialty market no one was targeting and set out to make it its niche. Residents living on an island not connected to the city by a bridge—they used a ferry service to commute back and forth—did not have access to fast-food delivery. The company set up a service that would allow it to cater to this niche market and arranged for fast-food delivery orders to be delivered by speedboat. Its niche marketing endeavor to a specialty market generated the interest of the residents and general public alike and received excellent media coverage. The fast-food company saw a need no one else was marketing to or servicing, and made it its niche. And the media saw a human interest story that would have appeal and turned out to cover the first delivery.

The same principles could be applied to the event planning industry. The florist who started out as an assistant to learn her trade began her business by doing floral arrangements for weddings. She began receiving requests to handle more and more of the decor elements and an event planning side of her company was born. Her floral displays attracted media attention and were featured in national magazines and on television shows. Demand for her designs came in from all over the world and she expanded into mail order. She was then approached about opening her own stores in a luxury hotel chain. Her business grew, meeting the needs of the professional market *and* the personal shopper.

Niche markets can also grow out of areas no one is rushing to take on. For years planners avoided getting involved in handling high school proms and have turned away any requests that came in. The prom market has now turned into a niche marketing opportunity that CNN reports brings in over US$2.7 billion in revenue a year, with the average couple spending US$1,200. Condé Nast recognized this growing segment and caters to this market with *Your Prom* magazine. Condé Nast found that the U.S. teen market spent over US$400 million a year on limousines and almost US$200 million on flowers. And proms and after-proms are becoming more professionally themed, as well. Parents and school faculty hope that by creating a memorable experience, students will stay longer at their supervised event. The students, through fundraising activities, usually raise money for decor and entertainment.

Some of the theme prom productions have rivaled what business corporations have done. Yes, special considerations go into planning a prom and making sure that everything progresses responsibly, with extra attention on drinking, guest safety, behavior and damage control. For an event planning company that focuses on social events, not corporate events, doing an outstanding job on specialty events such as a prom can serve to introduce it to a new audience. Being credited by having its company name on all printed material could lead to doing weddings, anniversary celebrations, bat and bar mitzvahs, sweet 16 parties, quinciñera (an Hispanic coming-of-age party for girls turning 15), debutante balls and baptisms, all of which can be very elaborate and big-budget parties, depending on the clientele. For example, one hotel catered a bris for 400 that was over US$200 a head.

One audiovisual company was surprised to find a niche market in handling the special needs of cemeteries, both in doing promotions for them and helping them with special arrangements for their customers. One event at a cemetery included a New Orleans jazz-style funeral procession using a marching band, which the audiovisual company arranged along with a memorial tape honoring the deceased. Traditional somber music was played at the beginning and at the end, but in the middle the music was more up-tempo, a lively celebration of life. The audiovisual company discovered that there were niche markets in themed send-offs, where funerals are personalized to celebrate the life of the departed. Theme funerals are a growing trend, as people are breaking with traditions. Instead of all-day vigils being held in funeral homes, receptions are being held in garden settings or private mansions, complete with food, beverage and entertainment. Art caskets, personal monuments—containing the ashes of the deceased—made for the backyard not the cemetery (they move with you) and even memorial T-shirts are some of the areas that have been developed to meet the needs of this new specialty niche market. What is important is that the theme funerals are handled with sensitivity and decorum, which is exactly what this audiovisual company did. In this case, the audiovisual company did not intentionally set out to create this niche market. The market found it, and the audiovisual company found out that a specialty market can be where you least expect it.

INCOME DRIVEN

Companies involved in the event planning industry often seek out their niche at opposite ends of the financial range. Some focus on meeting the needs on the high end while others put their energies on the moderate- to middle-income bracket. What is important to understand is that it does not necessarily mean that a corporate client with a million-dollar event planning budget is going to produce more profit than a client with a more modest budget. The margin of profit on high-end events is not always directly related to how much is being spent, and some companies choose to do these events for the prestige value it will bring them.

One event planning company created its niche by undertaking events that supported the arts. Its planners made knowing the ballet, symphony, opera and major works of art their passion. They did business with very influential corporate and society patrons who sat on the boards of directors for the arts. Working with those who had an appreciation for the finer things in life, it was important that they themselves and the staff they employed were schooled in the arts, fine wines, cigars, the choicest dishes to serve and what caliber of china they should be served on, as well as etiquette and protocol. When they held meetings in their boardroom, only the finest china and silver was used. Serving coffee or tea in foam cups or mismatched heavy mugs would be unthinkable for them and not in keeping with their image and the clientele they were cultivating. Their staff were always well dressed and they did not observe casual Friday. Many business and personal contacts grew out of the work they did for the arts and that spilled over into the business of designing events that would further support the arts. These would be paid for by corporate sponsorship and serve the dual purpose of promoting the corporate client and the arts through media exposure and the community's goodwill. For the corporate sponsor it was a marketing venture, not an event to be planned. The event planning company created its niche as being the link between the art world and the business community. With the success of the publicity from art-related events, the corporate clients then began seeking out the event planning company to handle their personal and business events as well. Instead of going the traditional route of cold calls, sales proposals and otherwise vying for business, the event planning company was able to make incredible business contacts in a different way. It targeted the upper-income bracket and met its prospects where they played to carve out its niche.

A new airline, wanting to create a niche market and stand out from its competition, does more than offer low fares to attract customers. Its customers are offered comfort as well as savings. Its planes are new, with leather seats and live satellite television for each passenger. Its service is excellent and the awards and accolades it has received include being one of the top five domestic airlines, the best low-cost airline, the best cabin staff in North America and airline of the year for 2003. Its targeted niche is servicing clients who want quality at affordable prices. With well over 16 million customers, it achieved its goal and a new fleet of aircraft has been ordered. It is expanding its business at a time when other airlines are going under. It found a niche and more than filled it.

Another airline has made a name for itself catering to the affluent market. When Britain began allowing dogs and cats from the U.S. and Canada to enter the country without the six-month quarantine, the airline got approval from the British government for a three-month trial to allow regular travel for cats and dogs on flights from Los Angeles to London's Heathrow Airport. If it proves profitable, this service will be extended to all its routes. It's not inexpensive and the pets travel not in their owners' lap but in cargo, but those who don't want to leave their pets behind now have an option. The service will hold appeal for the rich and famous, which is the airline's targeted market. It also offers beauty therapy, complete with massage, aboard its flights for its customers who like to be pampered. Also, its first-class passengers can eat what they like when they like, and mingle with other passengers at the onboard bar.

A very expensive restaurant that catered to the financial district lunch crowd looked to be uppermost in its clientele's mind when it came time to dine. It wanted to carve out a niche in an area where there was high competition for expense account lunches. It introduced after-work business classes in wine and food appreciation and brought in the experts. The classes were priced within reason and sold out immediately to up-and-coming executives looking for ways to give themselves the competitive edge and more business polish. The restaurant was fulfilling a need and doing so conveniently. Its intention was not to make money from this venture, but to introduce its services to new customers, and have them feel comfortable dining in the establishment and become known to the staff. As its peak business was through the day, with business meetings taking place over breakfast and lunch, the restaurant looked for ways to bring added marketability to itself by opening its doors to private evening events through the week and over the weekend. At night, its bar—located in a separate area—was busy until 6:00 p.m. when the city cleared out. Opening its facility to private events over the weekend brought in additional business from clients in the form of doing society weddings, engagement parties and other personal celebrations. The restaurant had a spectacular view of the city and lake, and corporate clients looking to impress their customers booked it for private events when firework displays were scheduled to take place. It was looking to be more than a possible place for lunch for its business crowd. It worked on building a relationship that went beyond that.

One decor company made no excuses for its rental prices. It had built a reputation of producing award-winning decor and designing events for big-budget clients—its niche. Being able to work with the funds to create spectacular results allowed it to show off its talents and win awards, which in turn helped to promote its companies. The planners also took on smaller events, but did not lower their rates because they knew that the quality of items they supplied was top-of-the-line in luxury. Event planning companies working in all budget ranges knew if they contracted decor through this company they never had to worry about the quality of items, such as linens, being used. The table settings would gleam and not one dish or glass would be chipped. The planners were artists with centerpieces and special effects. Catering to an upscale clientele allowed them to build a warehouse of quality goods that even companies with limited budgets looking for a touch of class could avail themselves of. Their appeal was enhanced by the awards they won, and the press coverage they received. That resulted from targeting their talents to a niche market that had a need to host events that left their guests impressed.

There are profitable niche markets on both ends of the financial scale, and they can expand into other areas. Do not limit your options by believing one has better possibilities than the other does. Examine them closely to see where they will lead you. In some cases, the two can even cross over as both you and your customer grow. For example, a men's retail clothing company turned its business into a US$1 billion business by making shopping at its stores less painful. Television sets turned to sports programs were staples in its stores, as were putting greens, foam footballs, pizza and donuts. It carved out its niche selling suits and is now moving into tuxedos, designer wear and sports clothes, and will be adding dry cleaning services to its facilities. It is projecting US$5 billion in sales over the next few years. It is growing with its customers and offering products that will meet their life stages, making the experience pleasurable and convenient. By adding dry cleaning and tuxedo rentals, it is creating opportunities to draw its clients back into its stores, which will lead to add-on sales and impulse purchases.

EMOTIONAL HOT BUTTONS

Emotional hot buttons address our wants, not our needs. They can be items or experiences that bring us pleasure, satisfy something inside of us or bring with it a certain cachet, such as being among the first to purchase one of the hottest items around. Placating an emotional hot button is what drives parents into a frenzy during the holiday season, waiting in line for hours, willing to pay any price for an item, trying their best to make sure that their children are not disappointed when they open their gifts and that their heart's desires, the season's most sought-after items, are sitting there waiting to be unwrapped. Reason sometimes goes out the window when people's emotional hot buttons are tapped—something those marketing their products to consumers know.

Emotional hot buttons come in many forms, and companies are making them their niche. They can be related to people, business, culture, fun, entertainment, personal desire, nostalgia, sports, environment and even pets. And sometimes when emotion is involved, price is no object. When tickets for the last flight of a Concorde went on sale, they sold out within an hour. Prices ranged from US$8,000 to US$10,000 one way. Being a part of history, no matter the cost, had value. It hit an emotional hot button.

Hotels looking to develop hot button niche markets are jumping on the pet-friendly bandwagon and rolling out the red carpet for their four-legged guests. Hotels are providing everything from special bowls for food and water, to plush designer doggie beds and chew toys. Some hotels are even offering special room service menus for pets, and depending on the category of hotel they are not inexpensive. At some luxury hotels, the doggy dinner menu selections can run as high as US$20. In order not to turn away future guests who may be allergic to pet hair, rooms are deep cleaned and vacuumed with a special filter so that incoming guests won't feel any discomfort. Upscale hotels and family-friendly hotels are both opening their doors to this specialty market, and it is proving to be very successful.

Major cities are tapping into the financial district's emotional hot button—the love of doing business over a game of golf. Business deals can be conducted over lunch in courses located minutes from the office. Membership for one New York facility is by invitation only and is reportedly starting at US$100,000. Golfers can get there in minutes by a fast ferry or there is a marina for private yachts. There is a definite cachet attached to being invited to play golf there, because of both the location and the course with Scottish-style links, which can be some of the most difficult to play.

One company tapped into people's secret desire to experience being a rock star and created an event that fulfilled it. It created a five-day fantasy music camp. More than 70 aspiring musicians signed up, from doctors and lawyers to everyday folk and even parents with their teens, in varying ages and musical abilities—to learn how to rock. They were divided into rock bands and taught by "counselors" (well-established names in the music business) to play two songs and have the chance to rock onstage.

Another company recognized the same emotional hot button but came up with something different. Its concept could be used as a team-building event, as opposed to the fantasy camp, which could be used as a stand-alone event for people to fulfill their individual passions or incorporated into an incentive program where camaraderie, not competition, would be the focus. This company was an entertainment company with its finger on the pulse of American culture, and had seen the public response to popular shows like *American Idol* that were attracting millions of viewers each week. People were watching others live out their musical dreams. Its answer was to create a niche, offering corporate clients a specialized team-building event that combined fun, fantasy, and learning something new, bringing their people together in a new way. Clients had the option of bringing in name performers to jam with their guests. It was successful at creating a niche, matching it with a corporate need and tailoring it to match its clients' budget.

A car company looking for a way to create an event that would both lure potential customers to attend and entice them to buy its new model cars knew it would have to do more than a traditional exhibit showcasing its new product. It knew that what holds the most appeal is actually sitting behind the wheel of the car. Getting the full experience of being able to touch and feel and truly envision themselves driving the car of their dreams would tap into their prospective customers' emotional hot button. The event planning company it worked with specialized in the automotive industry and it had made it its niche market. It annually did new car launches to dealers for several car companies, incentive programs for their car dealership sales staff and managed consumer events for them. It found a location that would hold great appeal, designed a show-stopping showroom and devised a way for attendees to be able to actually test-drive the cars in a contained area, ensuring that safety precautions and permit and insurance requirements were met. Its expertise and knowledge of the automotive industry and its customers helped it create the perfect hot button event for its client.

SPECIALIZED EXPERTISE

Individuals as well as companies can create their own niche. The success of the tenting company that also excelled at covering swimming pools came about because of the special talents of one individual. There are people that you come to depend on to handle special event planning needs. Planners will take these people around the world with them doing events because they have absolute faith in their abilities. For example, when you are doing special effects with pyrotechnics, are you going to trust your guest safety to someone you haven't worked with, or bring the people you know will do an outstanding job? The same applies to companies handling security. One security company is made up of ex-police officers, and they handle very-high-profile events without incident. The company has made guest safety its niche and hired staff that were professionally trained in all areas of law enforcement. It has marketed itself quite differently from a company that provides security by the hour, staffed by part-time workers with no formal instruction.

One event planning company employee carved out her niche by excelling in air transportation for groups of all sizes. Clients were thrilled with her service and how she handled their participants. She was doing something that she truly loved and for a company she enjoyed working with. Many tried to woo her away but she was not tempted. She also turned down opportunities presented to her to manage a branch office. It would take her away from what she did best and would put a cap on her income. She came up with a proposition to hire someone to handle her paperwork, allowing her to focus on negotiation, space management and customer service. But she wanted to pay for that person herself. Her reasoning was that if she simply had someone assigned to her that she would run into the possibility of having them pulled away to handle other tasks. By paying her salary and having the employee report only to her, she could make sure that she remained her employee's priority. She also wanted a computer at home that was networked to the office system. With four active children, there were times she needed the flexibility of being able to work from home. The company she worked with was open to trying her suggestion. She used her client appeal to create a job situation suited to her personal needs and a fit for the niche she had created. It became a very profitable venture for both the employee and the employer, as she was able to take on even more business.

Creating a niche by acquiring areas of expertise can result in building a demand for your services. It serves to increase not only sales but also personal and professional marketability. Just as a business can develop a niche market, as a professional you can carve out your own area of specialty in the industry. Many successful people in the industry made it their business to become the best in areas that would move them ahead, showcase their talents and create a need for what only they could produce.

Questions you can ask yourself to help you choose your niche include:

• What areas of expertise do I already possess that would meet an industry or client need?

• What specialty markets would be a match for the skills or interests I have?

- What attributes are required for the market I am targeting?
- What additional qualifications or characteristics would contribute to my success?
- Where do I see a business need that is not being met?
- Does this have the potential to grow into a viable market that I could service?
- Would this be a profitable venture?
- What are the long-term possibilities?
- What are the current emotional hot buttons in my field?
- Where have the most recent growth areas been?
- What has become obsolete?
- What sector is being overlooked by my competition and why?

PART 2

Market Development

The next three chapters cover the importance of defining who your client is, why targeting your talents helps to develop your market and how understanding and customizing customer service requirements can give you a competitive edge. These three key areas and the roles they play in market development are discussed from the event planning industry perspective and cover event planners, suppliers and their clients.

Many event planning companies and their staff, hot on their quest to secure new accounts, scrambling to research and develop numerous client proposals, and juggling the many demands of managing upcoming events never take the time to define their personal and company objectives. Caught up in the thrill of the chase and the invariable bidding frenzies that follow, most companies do not make the time to assess if the client they are pursuing will be an asset or a liability to them or their company. Without a clear vision of what your objective is and clarifying who your client is, valuable time, money, momentum and even reputation can be lost. This can greatly impede market development and professional business growth.

Once individual and company objectives have been established and desired client profiles prepared, energy can then be spent on targeting your talents in the right direction. Too often a shotgun approach is applied in the event planning industry, identifying—without qualifying—as many possible clients as possible and beginning pursuit hoping to hit a target. Efforts are fragmented and introductory proposals using form letters are ineffectual because time has not been spent on determining whether or not a potential client is a good match for your company and yours for theirs. Targeting your talents to the right audience and approaching them in a way that will get their full attention can give you a competitive edge in landing accounts. How to determine and identify the best client for your talents is covered in Chapter 4. Ways to take your marketability and apply it to market development are outlined in Chapter 5.

One size does not fit all when it comes to customer service. There is great value in discovering what each individual client requires. Standards of service can be the same but what is required and how these standards are applied can vary greatly from one client to the next. The attention to detail, accuracy, exemplary business behavior and other custom customer service principles hold true for a company or an individual. Understanding and customizing your clients' individual and company service requirements can save money, time and frustration on both sides. The questions to ask new and existing clients are discussed in Chapter 6.

4

DEFINING YOUR OBJECTIVE

Who Is Your Client?

Do you or your company have a criteria when it comes to soliciting sales from potential clients? One sales representative's only requirement was that a client be listed in the telephone directory. Precious person-hours were wasted as she worked her way from A to Z. And the time being wasted was not limited to the sales representative's. Office lines were tied up with outgoing and incoming calls and staff were constantly waiting for lines to clear. Administrative staff were coerced into "writing" form letters and preparing sales kits to be sent out to prospective clients who were never to be heard of again. Money was wasted on postage, envelopes, promotional material and long-distance calls. Caught up in day-to-day issues and putting out deadline fires, the company owner was unaware of the added stress and strain being put on his office staff. Tempers started fraying and the bills started coming in. How did this situation get so out of control? The salesperson was new and determined to make her mark. She had not been given company objectives regarding desirable clients and so set out to target everyone in her path. She failed to do preliminary research that would have eliminated the spending of time, money and energy on clients who had no intention of doing an event and were merely being polite when they told her to send her company information to them. Her intentions were good but she lacked direction on what type of client would be the best fit for her company.

At another company, the sales staff had to prepare prospective client lists and submit activity sheets that monitored their interaction with potential customers. While they had to be able to identify the type of customer they were chasing, the sales staff never had to explain why a specific client was on their list (e.g., they had a previous relationship with the decision-maker or the expertise to handle a certain account). When new sales staff were coming onboard, there was a mad scramble by existing staff to add more names to their list so that these clients would be inaccessible to the new salesperson as they "belonged" to someone else. The sales force became territorial and valiantly tried to defend any of the new additions to their lists. Wars between the incoming and existing sales staff were waged over who had closer ties to a potential client, even if that client was merely a known name, not a qualified company.

What these companies had failed to do was to define their company objectives, how they expected to achieve them and what client base they would require to do that. Sometimes event planning companies are so busy meeting the needs of their existing clients that they do not take the time to see if their clients are in fact meeting *their* corporate needs. Not all clients are created equal. Some will help you achieve your goals, while others take a stranglehold on your company and can drag you under. The shotgun approach of "targeting" anyone in their sights in the desire to land *any* account is frequently used, and it is only when a company becomes mired down with clients who turn out to be unprofitable do they stop to question their sales techniques and why they had ever actively sought and pursued these clients in the first place.

No one can sustain a business that is not set up to be profitable. One event planning company, whose resources were being drained by one of its clients that was expecting it to bankroll its payment as part of the terms of their contract, in desperation continually turned to one of its loyal customers to bail it out and help it make payroll and pay suppliers. The event planning company's demands on its long-standing client to pay more up front to offset the other client's deferred payments put a strain on the business relationship. In the end, the event planning company lost both clients, the one it could not afford to carry and the one it had alienated by taking advantage of its good nature. This also had a ripple effect on the office staff, who were aware of checks being held back to suppliers because of lack of funds and so on. This caused great apprehension about their own financial security, as staff worried about whether or not their own paychecks would clear.

You should not be doing business with a company that expects you to operate at a loss, carry them financially or have your sales force run amok, but that is exactly what some companies sign off on by not stopping to ask whether or not this is a company it really wants as a client. If companies and individuals do not take the time to define their objectives, weigh their options and make informed market development decisions, they can end up taking on more than they bargained for and that can lead to their downfall. One of the reasons why valued staff and clients quit on companies is because of ineffective market development and management. If staff are constantly overworked, staying late, spinning their wheels preparing proposals that never sell or managing clients that make the company no money, they will become disheartened and quit. And loyal clients, overlooked because other clients are draining the company with their incessant demands, can feel abused and look to find someone who will appreciate their business. Establishing business objectives and determining who the company's clients are enable the company to create the right type of environment for it to become successful and to be able to attract the staff with the right skills and levels of expertise required.

When defining short- and long-term business and professional objectives, there are several areas that must be reviewed, and they apply equally to employers, employees and clients. Take, for example, company growth. An employee who prefers working for a smaller organization may not be happy if the company starts to grow too rapidly. Similarly, some clients may prefer dealing with a smaller firm where they are the primary client, as opposed to being one of many, and may look elsewhere if the company's ambition is rapid growth. One event planning company lost long-term employees when it grew from a staff of six to more than 100 in a short period of time. The successful company bought a communications company to bring in an added dimension, but the two very different styles of operation did not mesh. The owner's attention was diverted to the new division on which he was not fully versed, and took major time away from running the other half of his business.

Money and time were poured into the new company but it was never as successful as his original concept. In the end, the owner had to sell and the company went through a third major change. Good employees and customers were lost.

The same skills the event planning community uses to create successful events can apply to defining objectives and finding the best client fit. They are:

- Visualization
- Research
- Development
- Planning
- Execution
- Reconciliation

VISUALIZATION

What do you envision to be the right size and style of company you want to create, work for or work with? Is it small, where everyone is familiar with all aspects of the company? Or is it much larger, with each section having its own area of responsibility, with little overlap? Will it require people with special skills or expertise? Do you see the office being one of many or a stand-alone operation? Where do you see the company headed five years down the road? Ten years? What role do you see yourself playing in the company's growth? How many quotes can you handle a month? How many events can you produce and direct? What kind of cash flow will you require?

In the exact same manner you visualize an event, visualize the location of the office, the commute and the parking. How large is the office and what costs are involved to rent it and run it? One very successful event planning company needed to be connected with a travel agency to handle its group tickets and offer reasonable travel rates, and have a boardroom for staff and supplier meetings and good parking. It didn't need a downtown location for its clients to come to it, because in most cases client meetings took place in the clients' offices. The owners knew that the dollars saved on expensive downtown rent could be applied elsewhere. They rented office space within an existing travel agency to give them a central base, but for the majority of the time their employees worked from their homes. Incoming calls were put directly through to the employees at home and clients never knew that the employees were not in the actual office. Employees were all very experienced in the field of event planning and did not require supervision or instruction, and met at the office when needed. The money saved on rent went into being able to afford to pay for staff who were fully qualified to work on their own, and a good telephone system and computer network. The office was located in an industrial part of town, which added to the rent savings. Their office structure fit their vision and their employees' lifestyle.

Another event planning company's vision was quite the opposite. The planners knew that with the audience that they were intending to market their services to, they needed to be at a prestigious downtown address. Their client base was in the downtown hub and they needed to be accessible to them at a moment's notice, without a lengthy commute. They also knew that they would need an office with a large boardroom, as well as space to entertain and impress guests. They invested time and energy in finding the right spot and used their event planning negotiating skills to hone an amazing long-term rental deal. Their location met both their vision and their budget.

For one event planner, the appearance of affluence would not have been appropriate for her image, personal beliefs and targeted client base. Her customers followed her from her previous employment and they knew she was just starting out. She had a reputation for being careful with their money and they expected her to do the same with her own. Her office was located in a strip mall and the furniture was eclectic, but fit the personality of the office, staff, owner and clients. She needed to impress her clients with her creativity, not her office address or furniture. Her clients' guests were very sophisticated and well traveled, and the events that they required had to be innovative and one of a kind. The money was better invested in the salaries of those who were masters in their fields, and a better office location and matching furniture could wait until the timing was right.

Three thriving event planning companies had three different visions, each having very specific requirements that needed to be met to help them develop their market and their company to its fullest. By using event planning visualization principles and applying them to the type of office they wanted to work in, the energy they needed it to have, and what they needed to make it work, they

were able to bring in exactly the right elements to make themselves successful.

RESEARCH

Market research is an important area that would never be overlooked when planning an event. It is where options are brought
into play, examined and either discarded or set aside for further
development. What needs to be considered in market research is
what area of the industry you will be focusing on, the prerequisites
of being able to work in a chosen area and what you bring to the
table. Do you know who your competition would be and the volume of business they do? Who are their customers? Have they
locked up the market or is there room for development? What
strengths do you possess that would set you apart from your competition and help you stand out? What need do clients have that is
presently not being met? Do you know who your potential clients
are? How can you help them to meet their objectives? How can
they help you to meet yours? Has the market you are considering
shown growth over the years or is it just holding its own? Is it profitable? Are the companies presently handling this type of business
struggling or do they show signs of prosperity?

One company hoping to set itself up to handle big-budget,
large-scale events knew that it would require someone proficient in
setting up custom computer systems to tailor them for its clients. It
needed to be a master of logistics and be able to comfortably work
with group sizes of over 2,000, and handle all of the intricate transportation and housing details. It also needed someone innovative
to bring new creativity to the event planning process. Once it had
the two key elements of logistics and creativity in place, it knew it
was ready to take on its competition and take over the market,
which it did. It was able to pinpoint a specific client need and
become the solution. Many companies in its field had strength in
logistics or creativity, but not one company was equally strong
in both. This company locked up the talent by offering them not
just a salary but shares in the company so that they had a vested
interest in staying and growing the business. When they started to
compete, their combined talents helped their company stand out
and be more marketable to their clients.

An independent entertainment marketer did his homework
and determined there was a need in his locale for a trusted local

entertainment source. He had an excellent ear, high standards and everyone he represented was reliable. Anyone he dealt with, from event planners to hotels, knew they could rest assured that the entertainers would show up at the event properly attired, prepped and well in advance of their contracted time. He made sure that his entertainers were cared for, and both they and his customers held him in high esteem. He thoroughly researched his market, found a need that he could fill and was very successful. Planners did not have the time to invest in sourcing out individual musicians and keeping on top of who delivered on-site. They needed a company they could turn to that could present them with options they could present to their clients, and that would always deliver a quality performance.

DEVELOPMENT

Are you fully qualified to service your proposed client base? Are there areas of development that could be explored to increase your marketability? Are there any learning curves to prepare yourself or your clients for?

What skills do you need to service your clients today? What skills do you need to service your clients tomorrow? Today, technology changes at the speed of light and it is no longer an option not to be tech savvy. For example, when online registration first was introduced to the event planning community, many held back and did not even take the time to investigate the pros and cons in order to be able to discuss its merits with clients if the subject came up. Event planning companies that embraced the technology and could offer their clients a means to custom reports, 24-hour access to their guests' RSVPs and a host of other improvements gave themselves a competitive edge over their competition. Are there skills and areas of development that could serve your targeted client better, put you or your company ahead of the competition and add to your marketability?

PLANNING

Once you have defined your objectives and identified your client, their needs and your needs, thought has to go into planning your next move. You do not want to play someone else's marketing game on the defensive and react to what the client or competition does, but rather create your own and plan for your success.

Who is your client? Where do you have a true possibility to be successful? One manufacturer put planners and suppliers that were willing to subject themselves to its bidding process through their paces. It had over 20 companies clamoring to propose and it was looking for a minimum of three destinations to be presented from each. It wanted payment concessions and cancellation extensions. It made constant changes, required numerous re-costings and would not pay more than 10 percent for management fees, which, when all was said and done, did not begin to cover the man-hours required to meet its very demanding needs. It had booked with the same event planning company for the past seven years and every year the same drama unfolded. Those bidding on the account were aware of the client's history but still wanted to have the opportunity to showcase their talents. The volume of work for event planning companies and their suppliers was intense and they knew going in that the odds were not in favor of their winning the account. The turnaround time was always tight and resulted in employees working around the clock, highly stressed, with all other work placed on the backburner. And for what? Very little in return revenue.

The downside of working with this account was the hours required to service it. The planners and suppliers invested time and money into researching and preparing the proposal, operating the file and servicing the client, but were not compensated by the return. In addition, those who were not successful in the bid lost time and money, but also endured added stress by putting their staff through unnecessary work. The companies bidding knew that the compensation did not match the effort, but they persisted year after year because they wanted the opportunity to gain experience of handling events in this field and they had no idea of how difficult the client actually was nor how little the return actually would end up being. One company that chose to decline bidding focused its attention on tapping into a new possibility that fit its desired client profile and its abilities. It scooped up a major high-profile event that gave it both prestige and profit. Everyone else had overlooked this opportunity while they were busy battling each other.

There are times when it pays off to challenge the competition and take on a new venture, but there has to be value in it to throw your hat into the ring. If it is going to divert your focus and not bring a return on investment, the decision to move forward needs to be questioned. A return on investment can be many things. It is not just based on money, and the cost must be weighted against the reward. If an event will fast-forward a company or an individual to a new level of skills or marketability, and it is on your planned path, it may be an investment you want to make.

EXECUTION

Can you deliver what your company promises and what your clients need? Is there anything that still needs to be developed—knowledge, skills or tools of the trade—to meet their expectations? If your objective is to do events for the fashion industry, for example, and this is the market you defined as the one you will be focusing your energies on, have you done all your homework before setting out to present yourself to potential clients? Do you speak their industry language and understand their event requirements? Do you know how to address their concerns? Are you up to date on new staging options, lighting and special effects? Do you know what the backstage requirements would be, whether electrical, mirrors or access to running water? If given the opportunity to bid and present, will you have covered all the bases or will you miss something and thereby show a lack of knowledge? Have you attended fashion shows to research presentation styles? Are you up on your designers? One top designer is a vegetarian, so to present an event with a menu based on meat would be a major faux pas. Do you know how to handle the security concerns related to the fashion industry, such as safety for VIP guests, and how to best deal with problems such as animal rights protesters? Are you proficient in handling the press? Do you have connections that would be an asset to the industry? Do you know how you are going to position yourself and how you stand out from your competition? Can you articulate your competitive edge to clients? Are you fully prepared to be the solution for the challenges your clients face? These questions need to be answered before you start to cold-call clients.

RECONCILIATION

The bottom line—profitability—comes into the decision-making process when you are defining your objectives and identifying your client. Are you embarking on developing a market that yields little return? If so, that will affect company growth, direction and expansion. Some events run at a loss, while others operate at a break-even point, allowing you no return to invest for yourself or your company. This could put you in a position of standing in quicksand. You may be afraid to make a move because you could go under and become unable to move forward. There has to be a return on the work being put forth because if you lose the ability to reinvest in yourself or your business you can lose the competitive edge.

If you find yourself mired in quicksand you need to be prepared to cut your losses quickly. It is not necessarily one industry or another that can affect your bottom line and stop you from achieving your definition of success. The bottom line can be money, time, and personal and professional satisfaction. It is different for everyone. For example, some event planning companies stay away from nonprofit events because they assume that there is no return, but that is not the case, as will be outlined in an upcoming chapter. Nonprofits are just another type of client.

One event planning company fired one of its clients because of the unreasonable demands the client was making on the planning company's staff. Morale was down and the time spent handling this client left the staff unable to solicit new business and service their existing clients properly. The cost of doing business with the client was too high, as it had the office running in circles, and while the company was a master of events it was unable to master this client. This particular client had a history of companies not wanting to work with it, and that should have been a warning sign. It also had a reputation for not paying its bills on time, putting planning companies at financial risk when the cancellation penalties on contracts they had signed with suppliers on their client's behalf became considerably higher than the money on hand.

Can you cope with a demanding client? What about a client that calls staff at home at midnight to propose changes? What about a client that won't pay its bills on time? What do you require from the clients you hope to do business with? Be very clear about this aspect when you are defining your objectives and identifying your client.

One Hawaiian hotel knew that to better service its clients in other time zones, it needed to have sales and service staff who were prepared to start their workday before the sun came up. The bulk of its business was not local and it knew that having sales staff on hand during its clients' operating hours would give it a competitive edge.

It met its bottom line in increased sales and profitability by hiring staff who were fully prepared to work early shifts (not extended days) to service its clientele. By doing so it knew that it could offer its clients something different. Having clients in different time zones and being able to meet their needs was not a problem for this hotel and a requirement it could easily fulfill.

Questions to ask yourself when defining your objectives and your client include:

- What size of company do I want to create or work for?

- How large do I want my company to grow or how large a company am I comfortable working for?

- How do I want the company I own or work for to operate? Is everyone involved in all aspects or is each area specialized?

- What are the hours of operation? Am I prepared to handle events at night and on weekends or do I strictly want to be involved in events that operate during the day through the week?

- Do I want to create events for the business, social, pleasure or nonprofit market?

- Do I want to do large or small events? What size event would I feel comfortable handling?

- Do I want to do events locally, nationally or around the world?

- Is there an industry that I want to specialize in?

- What would industry specialization require of me in the form of knowledge, skills and expertise?

- How do I define my role in the event planning industry—planner, supplier or client?

- Who would my competition be?

- What do I offer that would stand out and give me or my company a competitive edge?

- Where do I see myself five years from now? Ten years from now?

- What investments do I need to make now and in the future to take me to the next levels?

- What is my criteria for clients? What do I need and expect from them?

- Do I want to deal with one decision-maker?

- Am I comfortable dealing with decisions made by committee?
- Do I want to focus on large or small businesses or a mixture of both?
- What client type would my talents be the best match for?
- Will working with this client base be profitable?
- Do they pay their bills on time or do they have a reputation for being difficult?
- How can I protect myself from repeating any of my competition's mistakes in managing this type of client?
- Will working with this client be pleasurable?
- Will working with this client enhance my reputation?
- Will I be required to learn a new set of skills or invest in new equipment?
- Will I come away having learned something of value that could aid in meeting my objectives?
- How can I or my company be the client's solution?
- How am I best positioning myself to have maximum appeal?
- Are there special concessions that I have to be prepared to put in place?
- What are my areas of negotiation?
- What areas are non-negotiable?
- What value do I bring to my clients and they bring to me?
- Do I have any reservations about working with this type of company?
- What concerns could clients have about working with me?
- Are there any areas of conflict to consider?
- Will working in this field and with this client help me to reach my objectives, or move me away from reaching my goals?
- Are there any spin-off opportunities? (For example, will planning an event locally for a company branch office for little or no profit open the door to handling their company's business internationally?)
- Will working with this client help me to develop my market and add to my marketability?

5
TARGETING YOUR TALENTS

Unlike many professionals like architects, doctors or lawyers that require a fee or retainer up front from clients, event planning companies hoping to land an account are asked to absorb real hard costs in the form of money and labor. Event planning companies are asked to pull out all the stops in creativity and design on speculation, without any guarantees or compensation. Some do so willingly time after time, jumping into the bidding brawl, without questioning whether or not they would be further ahead if they declined an invitation to bid.

Planners position themselves as a service industry, as opposed to being professionals in the business of motivation, and generally are uncomfortable asking to be paid for their expertise. It is the same dilemma that travel agencies, car dealerships and the like deal with. Customers come into their offices asking for expert advice, which is freely given, with no guarantees that the client will buy from them. Yet these same customers would not expect to dine in a restaurant, golf or see a movie without being asked to pay.

Anyone visiting a doctor knows that there is a cost for his or her services and that a hiring a lawyer will usually require payment of a retainer, but this is an expected and accepted practice because they are paying for professional advice.

Planners' expertise in producing an event that will generate dramatic returns is an important tool to corporations. Event planning companies play a vital role in their customers' sales and marketing campaigns and when the events are done right they have a direct impact on a company's success and bottom line. The sheer volume of work that goes into the research and development of a proposal, the substantial costs, and the risk of failure have to be carefully weighed when committing to bid on a project. The cost of time, money and energy on the part of the event planning company and its suppliers has to be reviewed before moving ahead and giving away creativity and professional advice.

Some companies have no conscience when it comes to soliciting ideas, using the submitted bids as a fishing expedition for concepts and costs, then doing them in-house. Savvy event planning companies are starting to employ new bidding tactics and valuing the vital role they play in their clients' growth, and are not worried about what their competition is doing—they are doing what is best for their company. Some event planning companies have begun charging a non-refundable retainer to cover bidding costs, and this fee is then applied towards the cost of the event should they be awarded the business. If the company requesting the bid declines to pay a design fee, it is prepared to walk away, most likely having come out ahead in savings of its time, energy and money, having not spent them on what could have merely been a company's attempt to meet its bid quota. It chooses instead to turn its attention to finding clients who value what it has to offer. Others are investing in themselves and their business and targeting their talents to specific clients, declining to take part in a bid situation. Experience has taught them that if they focus their energies in a specific direction the rewards can be much greater. They are looking for clients that meet their needs and whose needs they can meet, as opposed to jumping on the bidding bandwagon and trying to be a jack-of-all-trades.

> **T I P**
>
> Look at how your customers do business. Do they bid on speculation? Is there a charge for their services? Knowing how their business operates is important. If they do not operate their company on a system of providing information for free but for a fee, but are asking your company to do that, this should be taken under consideration when deciding whether or not to incur the costs for bidding.

One company was very successful in meeting its own and its clients' needs. It was determined to carve out its niche in the wedding planning market, which suited its nature and talents. In the beginning, its planners tried juggling corporate clients with their wedding clients but found that the two were incompatible. Their wedding clients needed their attention day and night, but they did not begin to work with them until their services were retained. Their corporate clients, on the other hand, made heavy deadline demands with no guarantee of business in return. They decided to focus their attention on wedding planning, which held less financial risk but required more personal attention. When they sat down and worked out how many weddings they could handle each week, they took into account that their clients would require their physical presence at rehearsals as well as their assistance in overseeing the event.

Corporate clients place their trust in the planner's sales representative and the team he or she puts together. With weddings, the bride and groom want the person who has orchestrated the actual events to be with them, as there is an emotional connection that has developed, and they depend on them to see them through their special day. The wedding planners knew their financial objective and determined their minimum management fee. When potential clients called they were told about their fee structure and no time was wasted trying to cajole couples who could not afford their services to book with them. Their intention was never to put a customer or their business in a position of debt. They made a professional decision and a business decision to target their talents to upscale society weddings. Having made that decision they then could focus their energies on making themselves the preferred wedding planner of their target market. They were able to define the attributes that they would need to bring forth to woo and wow their chosen clientele.

They knew that if their clients felt valued and cared for that they would be loyal and that loyalty would lead to profits, referrals and spin-off business. They also felt that their business could expand by being available to their clients for all the special events in their lives—baptisms, anniversaries and special family celebrations—handling every stage of their customers' and their family and friends' life cycles. They knew that they had to use emotional marketing in their promotional endeavors. They treated their clients as carefully as they would million-dollar clients right from the very beginning because they realized the potential value of each customer. The clients they marketed to were all in the upper-income bracket and an anniversary party could easily cost over US$100,000. They charged a minimum management fee to handle any event and the same fee applied even if they were planning an intimate themed Valentine's celebration for two. The cost of acquiring new clients was high and they felt the time they invested was worthwhile, as the effort they put forth in the beginning could be long lasting.

The wedding planners understood that to penetrate their market they needed to connect with their target customer face to face, and decided to spend their time, energy and money attending and contributing to gala fundraising events. They volunteered their creative services to boards of directors in exchange for company credit on promotional material and complimentary tables at events, and worked tirelessly to produce outstanding events on behalf of charities so that their company name and reputation would become known. Gala fundraisers were the perfect vehicle to showcase their creative talents, budget management and event orchestration, as well as network with society patrons—their potential client base—both on the committees and at the events. They were careful to limit their involvement to that of event design consultant, available only to select head committee members and event chairs, so that their time spent volunteering did not affect their business or level of service to their clients (e.g., they did not spend time selling tickets or asking for donations from suppliers for items for the silent auction—those activities they left in the hands of the volunteers). They made sure that their contribution was at a level that matched their skills, would be of great value to nonprofit organizations and would serve to get them noticed. They were actively involved in overseeing event set-up but also made sure that when events started they were able to act as guests, mingling and mixing, as opposed to being tucked away behind the scenes with the staff they brought in to aid volunteers with the actual logistics. Having negotiated tables at events in exchange for their consulting advice allowed them to invite select guests to see their creativity firsthand, and being thanked on stage added to their promotion. They also worked with the media to make sure that they were looked after, the proper pictures were taken and that they had copies for their files along with print material crediting them with event design and orchestration. They made sure that the media knew the role they played in each event's success and their company was often mentioned in newspaper write-ups or captured on film for the nightly newscast, taking reporters for an exclusive behind-the-scenes look at preparations.

Their credibility grew and the positive publicity they received served to increase their marketability. The money and time they invested in becoming a trusted resource was more valuable in terms of promotion than taking out an ad in the newspaper or sending out promotional kits on speculation. They also delivered to their clients by exceeding their expectations, which served to enhance their reputation. They always made clients feel cared for, gave them what they needed and provided them with options that would meet their future event planning needs. The wedding planners also never lost sight of the fact that the actual weddings and the festivities leading up to them would also serve to showcase their talents to potential lifelong clients (wedding guests) as well.

MATCHING YOUR TALENTS TO YOUR AUDIENCE

Targeting your talents to your audience involves using many of the same essential skills planners use to create an event. The trick is applying them differently and using them as a means to market and promote yourself and your business and for client acquisition, client referral and client retention. These include:

- Evaluation
- Examination
- Development
- Strategy
- Innovative Design
- Personalization
- Fulfillment
- Prioritization

EVALUATION

When you have defined your personal and company objectives and identified your desired—not targeted—client base, the next step is evaluation. What talents do you or your company possess? Make a list of your assets. These can be based on natural talent, skills, specialized knowledge, equipment, location, staff, present clients, connections and any other defining feature, such as multilingual staff or any attribute that would be of value to clients. Next, make a list of both the known and perceived needs of the clients you are seeking to do business with or market yourself to.

Sample List—Personal Assets

Analytical in nature.

Can easily handle logistics for up to 2,000 guests.

Special skills in handling automotive, financial and entertainment industry.

Has done events around the world. Well-schooled in protocol and customs.

Extremely creative. Has often been the first to introduce a new event element.

Specialized knowledge in special effects, audiovisual and stage production.

Proven history of designing events that strategically meet all of the client's objectives.

Dead-on accuracy with costings. Event reconciliation always on target or under budget.

Excellent negotiation abilities.

Experienced in business development, creative design, event management and on-site production.

Adept at handling media event requirements.

Experienced at orchestrating charity event and silent auction setup.

Sample List—Perceived Needs of New Target Market (e.g., Nonprofit Gala Fundraisers)

Good direction to volunteers who may have little or no experience in event planning.

Availability for meetings. Many could be at night due to volunteers' work schedules.

Skilled negotiator in obtaining donated goods.

Good business contacts (e.g., able to obtain a car for a charity raffle).

Ability to provide budget updates on a regular basis.

Staff to handle the RSVPs.

Media contacts.

EXAMINATION

Examine the two lists carefully and objectively. Assess whether there are any gaps between the two lists. In the above example, being able to handle media requirements at an event is very important, but not the same as having personal media contacts you can call and persuade to cover the event. Determine whether or not you can provide exactly what your clients will require and if so at what level. For example, you may say straight off that you are not prepared to solicit silent auction donations from what could someday be your potential clients, but that you are prepared to give suggestions to the volunteers. Or, if there is a match of interests, put forth a suggestion, such as approaching a car company that may be seeking promotion of a new product for a car to raffle. Do you meet their basic requirements or do your abilities more than meet their needs? Is there a good match between what you have to offer and what the client will require of you? Are there any red flag areas showing up that cause concern, such as the time that may be required to train the volunteers or the number of meetings you may be required to attend? Social elements of meetings, delayed start times and off-topic conversations can be circumvented by meeting with the board and committee heads. Each nonprofit organization is different but should be examined as to how their meetings are run to see if there is a fit.

DEVELOPMENT

What areas stand out as requiring development to move you into a better marketing position? Attach a value to what would be required to bring you or your company up to the level it needs to be operating at to provide you with a competitive edge and help you to stand out from the competition. One event planner who was actively seeking to do business with nonprofit organizations did not let an organization's need for someone to handle RSVPs for a large affair phase her. She knew it would be disruptive to have the calls come into her office so she simply outsourced to a service that would do it for her and put in a dedicated line for the calls. The cost was minimal when compared to the stress it would have placed on her office staff. The client and the event planning company were best served if they focused their attention on planning the event, not taking the RSVPs. Do due diligence and then decide whether or not it is worth the investment of time, energy or money to you. Based on where you are today, your desired clients' requirements and what will be required of you developmentally, is this still a client base you wish to move forward in and actively pursue at this time? Are you prepared to give your full commitment to this undertaking?

In the above wedding planning company example, the planners knew that they had to develop their contacts and that initially it could require a major time commitment from them. They were prepared to give up personal time to make their company's name known in new circles. They also knew that it was not a long-term commitment because once they had established the name and their credibility, the time spent making new contacts would lessen.

They would eventually be in a position to shift gears and be selective about which gala events they volunteered their services to, and would look at supporting other fundraisers in different ways, such as by purchasing tables, making donations, or providing a free wedding planning consultation as an item in a silent auction, that would still garner them goodwill publicity.

STRATEGY

These two sayings—"plant seeds in soil not sand" and "fish where the fish are"—have particular meaning when considering strategy. If you plant seeds in sand they will not grow; they require rich soil to flourish. If you fish where fish are not biting, at the end of the day you have nothing, or, in fishing terms, you have been skunked. You need to spend your time where the fishing environment is plentiful. To give yourself or your company a competitive edge you need to create a marketing strategy that is environment rich. By volunteering for and attending upscale gala fundraisers, the wedding planners put themselves in an environment rich with potential. They were targeting the society market and knew they needed to be in target-rich surroundings. They were planting seeds in soil not sand, and fished where the fish were. They were meeting their clients where they lived and played. They didn't spend their money or time taking out booths at bridal shows or expos—that wasn't their targeted audience, and they wanted to focus on quality not quantity. They also wanted to work with big budgets and special effects.

For someone else, a bridal show could be the perfect vehicle. One multi-million-dollar event planning company started exactly that way. Its planners started out doing tabletop centerpiece arrangements. Their strategy was quantity and quality in design, not price, and their product was affordable to all income levels. The bridal shows brought them visibility. Their work was very different and received rave reviews. Their time spent at trade shows was not wasted, as it also provided them with a means of learning new trends and making industry contacts. They expanded their knowledge and then expanded their services to include linens, chair covers and place setting rentals. From there, they worked with event planners and paid attention while they were doing event setups, and went on to master event design. They had the opportunity to see how different decor and event planning companies operated and learned as much as they could on the job about their business. They knew they had the creativity, expertise and experience to offer their customers something fresh, and they moved forward to become a very successful full-service event planning company.

INNOVATIVE DESIGN

Just as people move through life stages and lifestyles, so do companies. When you are targeting your talents to your client you not only have to look at where *you* will be in five or 10 years but where *they* will be as well. How will you or your company keep up with their changing needs? What will you need to do to keep pace?

One event planning company lost a client of long standing because it refused to grow with the client's technology needs. The client was a leader in its field and its events had to be cutting edge. When the client's competition began offering its guests online registration and the planning company was still sending out invitations by mail and the only means of responding was via return mail or telephone, the client felt that it was falling behind. The client wanted to provide its guests with access to the latest innovations, to be able to have customized Web pages that featured event information and to have the capability to send out updates. Its event planning company did not take its requests seriously and instead clung to the way it had always done business. The event planner and customer grew apart and the client moved on to a company that could meet its needs of today, not just yesterday.

Another company took a different tactic. It designed its company to be the one leading its customers forward. It offered innovative solutions to needs its customers had not yet identified. Its planners made sure that they kept current, attended educational seminars and brought in one-on-one training that would enhance their personal and professional abilities. They gave themselves a competitive edge by growing and expanding their talents to meet the future needs of their clients. Their objective was to not stagnate and they knew the clients they had aligned themselves with shared the same ideals. They wanted to be the one to stand out in their industry, setting the pace and leading the way.

PERSONALIZATION

How can you or your company help build your client's company? How can you gain your client's trust? One way is by personalizing your service and understanding each client's perception of value. This can affect their willingness to remain loyal. They need to feel commitment, not just to their event but to their success. Look for ways to target your talents to meet each client's individual needs and look for ways to develop superior value.

One client who had been badly burned on budget mismanagement by one event planning company valued transparency highly. He was leery about dealing with event planning companies that refused to divulge how the costs were broken down and only presented "packaged costs," which is where costs are not itemized but lumped together as a per-person charge (e.g., $250 per person as opposed to breaking out how that figure was arrived at). The event planning company that won his trust and his business did so by creating a cost summary that was laid out menu-style, with each cost itemized and backup provided without being requested. He delivered exactly what his client valued most. Price was not the determining factor in the selection process, but finding a company whose business ethics mirrored the client's was.

FULFILLMENT

Devise a way to deliver more. The "more" should be targeted to what has value for individual customers. It does not have to be a monetary expense. One decor company made it a point of delivering more than its clients expected whenever it could. If it had props sitting in its warehouse that would enhance the event, the decor company would contact the planner the day before the event and offer to have additional props brought in at no additional expense. The props were just sitting in the warehouse, it was too late for someone else to rent them and the company had room on the truck and staff available to assist with the setup.

It would never presume to bring extra material without first checking with the event planning company. Its reasoning was twofold. First, its staff knew that planners don't like to be surprised. There may be times when extra splash would not be appreciated, for example, if an event planner's client was looking to keep its event low scale so that its staff would not think that company money was being spent unnecessarily if times were tight. The second reason was marketing. They were able to make offers to their clients, the event planners, which showed that they were concerned with making their events as successful as possible, and they gave the planners a chance to look good to their clients. By calling their clients with the offers the decor company made, the planners could demonstrate their strong relationship with their suppliers and the extra value they could bring to their clients. By delivering more for their client, the decor company positioned itself in a favorable light and gave planners the same opportunity to do so with their clients.

PRIORITIZATION

Targeting your talents to your audience means selling what clients are buying. Knowing exactly what that is is a priority. What you are selling is your creativity, knowledge and motivational expertise in being able to strategically design events that achieve client goals, and it must be a fit for a buyer. Top precedence must be given to looking at ways to develop and capture your market.

What happens when the market you want to develop is not located in your backyard? Some companies shy away from creating their niche internationally. They have the talent to create and produce extraordinary events but the location in which they live is not a target-rich environment for this market, so their plans for further development fall by the wayside. For example, if what you truly want to do is be a part of designing high-profile events, such as glittering movie premieres and high-society events, a target-rich environment would be Los Angeles, New York, Washington D.C., Toronto, Vancouver, London, Cannes or another major city. If you live in a small town, creating the same type of market would be difficult, because the number of events of this caliber and budget could be limited. Does this mean that you either have to give up on your dream clients or move? No. Many meeting, incentive and special event planning companies market their talents and services successfully to customers around the world and do not limit their options to local clientele.

For years, planners have proposed events in locations that no one in the office may have traveled to yet. The in-depth research that goes into preparing a proposal, added to years of experience, enables event planning staff to be able to do this successfully. The first time people from the office may actually see the site is when the proposal is sold and they go on a pre-site inspection, arriving at the designation in advance of their client in order to do a quick review and familiarize themselves with the location before conducting the formal site inspection. Site inspection staff will set off with video and digital cameras in hand to capture all-important elements for the operations department back home. They will film the carpeting, the wall coverings, the ceiling fixtures, room layout, doorways, hallways, stage sightlines and room barriers such as columns so that those operating the program will have a visual walk-through of the property. They will gather menus, sales kits and whatever else is relevant to the event logistics. They are completely comfortable planning, operating and executing events from afar.

Experienced planners are equally skilled in soliciting and servicing clients long distance. Location does not have to be an obstacle. You may be required to fly in for the presentation and a series of face-to-face meetings as the planning for the event progresses, but these costs can be included in the event budget if the fit is right. With today's technology, where you live does not have to be a liability if you have something unique to offer your clients. One North American company known for its imaginative events created a very inventive incentive for a company based in England. Its planners had been at the same resort as their future client earlier in the year, and observed what their program included and how it was run. They saw a match in business and creative styles, and knew they could offer the customer much more than they were presently receiving in terms of design and service. They contacted the client after both programs had finished—to solicit sales on site would have been a breach of business etiquette and ethics—about the possibility of handling their account and were given an opportunity to fly over and present. They captured their client with their creativity, their history and their ability. Being an ocean apart was of no concern and they established a long-term working relationship.

> **T I P**
>
> Conceivably, two or more event planning companies could be running events simultaneously at a hotel or other large venue. Clients will take note of how someone else's event is being run and have been known to ask for business cards from companies that impress them. One client was shocked to find its competition had better quality transportation and better positioning of the waiting vehicles at the airport. The client had prided themselves on being number one in their business, but that day their sales force had to walk by the "little guy" in their industry to get to their motorcoaches, which were visibly not up to the standards their competitor was using, and carry their own luggage while the "little guys" settled into their comfortable seats, leaving their luggage to the baggage handlers. The company executive made it a point to find out which event planning company was offering superior service.

Another event planning company had similar success orchestrating conferences for physically challenged individuals, such as those hearing or visually impaired. The planners had developed the skills required, and having mastered their market set out to introduce themselves to special needs companies such as associations and schools that could benefit from working with them regardless of where they were located. They made it their priority to market their skills to this select group and made a name for themselves in the process. For example, when a group of visually impaired participants wanted to climb the Acropolis, the planners knew exactly what would be required to allow them to do so with comfort and ease of mind regarding their safety. As they stood at the top, bystanders were awed with the care they saw given to the participants. Word of mouth spread around the world and clients began actively seeking them out. They had developed their skills, targeted their talents to one specific market and found by doing so that as they built their company, they also built their reputation as industry experts who were in demand, regardless of their location. Another event planning company whose staff were all pet lovers made pets their special interest target, and handled dog shows and related events as well as other types of animal competitions across the country.

Look at what you have to offer clients and market yourself accordingly. Don't rule out potential clients based on location or even company size—yours or theirs. If you are a small business, never be intimidated about approaching clients who may seem out of your league if you have something special to offer them.

One independent planner landed major accounts that many large event planning companies would have loved to have. He designed and orchestrated outstanding events for his clients while sitting in his backyard, not an office. He was an event planning company of one, and where and how he conducted his business did not matter. His clients were buying his creativity, designs, expertise and reputation, not his office space. He never met many of his clients in person until the advance setup of the event. Business was successfully conducted over the telephone, and via courier and e-mail. His events delivered. He had a keen understanding of each one of his clients' objectives and targeted his event designs to meet them. He was not a party planner; he was a motivational master with a fresh take on how his clients could improve their business and a proven history of results. That is how he marketed himself to clients and won over their business. The incentive events that he created were so unique and so on-target that he motivated his clients' sales staffs to produce outstanding results. As sales went far beyond their wildest expectations, the clients ended up having to send back-to-back groups to reward events, as they had more people qualifying than available hotel rooms. In short, he was a master of strategic event planning. Strategic event planning is discussed in great detail in *The Business of Event Planning: Behind-the-Scenes Secrets of Successful Special Events* (John Wiley & Sons, 2002).

Questions to ask yourself when targeting your talents include:

- What are my areas of expertise?
- Where do I need to improve?
- Which clients would most benefit from my skills?
- What are these clients buying?
- What am I selling?
- What are my customer criteria?
- What are the customer's criteria?
- Are we a business match?

- Are there any additional skills, knowledge or equipment that I will require to service this type of client?
- How will I be able to contribute to my client's success in a way that is different from anyone else?
- How can I create new value for my client?
- What do I bring to clients that is new, fresh and innovative?
- In what areas can I provide my customers with more than they expect?
- How can I display my talents to capture my market?
- What marketing and promotional opportunities exist?
- What will get my clients' attention?
- In what target-rich environment am I likely to find my clients?
- What will be required of me or my company to keep pace with my clients' growing needs?
- Will working in this area bring me job satisfaction?
- Is this a profitable market to pursue?
- Am I marketing my talents to an industry that holds longevity or will it dry up quickly? Where will this industry be in five or 10 years?
- In what direction will developing this market lead me?
- Are there cross-selling or spin-off sales opportunities in this field?
- What other opportunities exist in this market?
- Is this market compatible with my existing client base?
- What investments in time and money will I have to make to develop this market?
- How long will it take me to make inroads in this market area?
- What are the risks of pursuing this market?
- What are the rewards of working in this field?
- What do I require from my customers?
- What will my customers require from me?
- What will I learn from working in this market?
- What is the volume of work that will be required?

- What do I need to put into place to be able to successfully manage the work?
- What will give me a competitive edge?
- How can working with me give my clients a competitive edge?
- Is what I am doing part of my overall personal and professional business plan?

6

CUSTOMIZING CUSTOMER SERVICE REQUIREMENTS

Too often companies blanket customer service, applying one standard of customer service generally without exception, and neglect to individualize it to actually meet the service requirements of each customer. They make the common mistake of calling their company standards "customer service." Having high company standards and maintaining them is an important element in customer service because it ensures consistency and conveys to the client a sense of order. But company standards tell a customer the level of service at which their needs will be handled, not how their distinctive requirements will be met. For example, a company's standards may decree that its telephone always be answered by the third ring and in person. This company standard may have been set to demonstrate its efficiency to incoming callers, as well as show its customers that their calls are important. The customer knows that what they are experiencing when they contact the office is exactly what *their* guests calling in will encounter. How the telephone is answered, how the caller is transferred to another line and how they are put on hold may be another company standard, and one that can help companies to stand out with their polish and professionalism.

Office dress, codes of conduct, and correspondence protocol all fall under company standards, and the standards companies put in place can set them apart. It is important that policy and procedures be in place so that everyone has a clear understanding of what is and is not acceptable business behavior, and so that everyone is operating from the same page. Once established, company standards are the foundation on which to build a powerful level of customer service.

Just as no two special events are alike, no two customers' needs will be exactly the same. It would be unthinkable for an event planning company that is selling its creativity to produce canned programs. If a company did, it would not be meeting its clients' objectives, as each event must be tailor-made to address specific client concerns. The medium may be the same, for example, you may use the same venue a number of times or the same destination or the same event planning principles, but the message, how it is applied and the means of delivery is what makes the difference and makes each event unique.

Just as canned events do not succeed in meeting customer requirements, so will offering canned customer service. Having only one service method in place to handle diverse customer needs is akin to producing canned events. Companies not taking this into account leave themselves open to having their customers easily courted away by other companies that demonstrate that they are more in tune with their industry's distinctive requirements and their individual company needs.

You only need to recall your own experiences of being frustrated with a supplier who displayed no understanding of how your business operates, or whose staff would not make the effort to look for areas of compromise that would serve both of you better, to know how being the recipient of canned customer service feels. What you surmised at that time, and rightly so, was that true customer service was a foreign concept to that supplier, and what they were offering was merely lip service. When faced with non-existent customer service from their suppliers, planners have no compunction about looking for new sources. They know that if their needs are not being met, then their customers' needs won't be either. For example, an event planning company requested that the payment dates on its client's contract be adjusted to accommodate the client's company check run. To have checks cut manually was not a simple procedure and the event planning company was bringing this forward at the time of contracting, anticipating no objections as the dates only had to be adjusted by a matter of weeks, not months. This is not an unusual customer service request in the industry, nor is it unreasonable. It is normally easily accommodated, so the request for a change was not brought up after the fact. The supplier—after the client went through several levels of being passed around—stated that its company policy was that the payment dates had to remain as is and that it would not consider making a change, so the event planning company and client did. For the event planning company and its client, the lack of customer understanding and service was a deal breaker. They decided that if the supplier was that uncompromising before contracting, they might end up with buyer's remorse if they continued with them. Instead, the event planning company found an alternative supplier that offered similar product, price and most importantly superior customer insight and service. For this supplier, adjusting the payment schedule was a matter of course, not concern, and it won the account over with its customer service.

Understanding and customizing customer service requirements involves mastering the Es of exemplary personalized customer service:

• Expectation

• Excel

• Embrace

• Enlighten

• Educate

• Enrich

• Energize

• Excite

• Environment

• Employees

- Efficiency

- Evaluate

- Ethics and Etiquette

EXPECTATION

Companies tout their unsurpassed levels of customer service to buyers in letters of introduction, client proposals and presentations, hoping to convince them to do business with them. But the outpouring of empty promises has become meaningless and does little to impress potential clients. Exactly how your level of customer service is going to help them succeed in their company mission is what clients want to know. They don't want to be placated by fluffy phrases filled with standard fare.

Companies have their own definition of customer service and what it means to them. When a customer agrees to contract a supplier's services, both parties are filled with high expectations. Seldom are these expectations voiced by either side, so as they begin their working relationship neither side has a true understanding of what the other requires, each expecting the other to be proficient at mind reading. And often the end result is disappointment on both sides, as their expectations remain unfulfilled.

Customer service, although often forgotten, is a two-way street. In order to satisfy customers' needs and meet their expectations, you must first be able to identify them. Second, action plans must be developed in order to fulfill the needs one by one. Every business has its own intricate set of requirements that are common only to it. For example, one car company required its event planning staff to be available after hours to answer questions from its head office, which was located overseas. Every evening, the car company executives spoke with their higher-ups, updating them on their event's progress. Questions would be asked that required immediate answers, so having someone at the event planning office to field their calls at this time was an important customer service requirement for them. This might not be necessary for another car company, which might have its own unique and important customer service requirements. Knowing what these requirements are plays an important role in being able to customize your service to your client. But that is only one part of the service equation.

Within each industry, each individual company has its own methods of conducting business.

For example, if you specialize in handling events for the financial industry, there are a number of elements you'll discover on your fact-finding missions that will be common to each of the financial companies that you work with. If you are doing events out of town, it is important to make sure that certain newspapers like *The Wall Street Journal* are made accessible to attendees, that attendees have a central message board set up and that if an urgent call comes in for an attendee, he or she is found immediately. These are expectations of customer service that a financial company might have. How these expectations are managed can affect event costs—for example, you may need to bring in additional people to staff a message center—but you can easily manage them if you know about them before the event takes place. If due diligence was not done beforehand and this was not discovered until the group was on site, to meet the client's customer service level expectations could mean having to pull staff members off other duties, potentially affecting program operations. Items such as special newspaper requests and message boards may not occur to someone who hasn't worked in this market before and may be easily overlooked. They are not necessarily items that would be spelled out in the contract, for example, many hotels will provide a specific newspaper at no additional charge if asked or it may be included as part of the negotiations with the hotel. Event planning companies bidding on financial business, having done their homework and researched customer service expectations in this industry, can use this knowledge as a marketing tool.

In their presentations to clients, they can include specific mention of these customer service features, which will give them a competitive edge by demonstrating an understanding of their industry. But event planning companies must be prepared to delve deeply into each company's expectations. One financial company's customer service expectations included provisions being made for the president's small children and nanny who were accompanying him, and they counted on their event planning company to cater to them at all times. Another financial company's customer service expectations included having someone in the office at 7:00 a.m. to be available to its staff at the start of their day and ensuring that all promotional mailings related to its event reached its offices in time to be collated with its participants' other mail to minimize delivery costs. If the material did not arrive at its offices in time, it expected the event planning company to pick up any additional mailing costs. Same industry, two customer service issues that were the same and two that were worlds apart.

It is imperative to sit with clients and determine their customer service needs before making promises that may not be met. Promises to customers regarding their customized service requirements impact staff, and must be taken into account. Can you deliver what the client is looking for and if so how? If the client has unreasonable expectations or those that will incur extra cost, then this needs to be dealt with up front to avoid feelings of disappointment and letdown on both sides.

EXCEL

What does customer service mean to you? Appraise your current levels of customer service and determine what holds value to specific customers. List common areas where you excel. These can become key selling features when they are combined with personalized customer service. Again, don't confuse company standards with customer service. They are two different areas.

One company excelled at anticipating its clients' needs. It researched the industry its clients worked in and reviewed client history with past suppliers, looking for areas where it could step in and meet its clients' needs in advance. It also kept very detailed notes on what transpired on site and made sure that past requests were reviewed so that it could be prepared for the next event. Its clients' special customer service requests varied. One client had a company president who would not go on stage without having a special brand of hair gel. Having spent one frantic Sunday morning scouring the city before his presentation, the planning company's staff resolved that as part of their customer service to this client they would always come prepared to meet his very special need. The next year the same request came in, and within minutes, they were able to produce his required product, and the event went on without any delays or unnecessary stress. It was a small thing to remember and one that required little effort to secure in advance. But to their client it displayed a company that excelled at caring about the details that they personally required to make their event a success.

One event planning company had a client who loved to do intimate client appreciation events for its customers and their partners. It traditionally held a cocktail reception and dinner followed by an evening at the theater or another high-profile event, and made sure that its guests were seated in the best seats of the house. The event planning company knew that having the best possible seats available was what was most important to its client, to its company image and its staff's personal reputations, and made it its priority to stay on top of what was coming into the city. Often the event planning company, through connections it developed, was able to secure tickets for the best seats in advance of announcement to the public, and the client was ecstatic to have the offer presented and would immediately contract for the event. As a result of purchasing so many high-priced tickets throughout the year, the event planning company was often offered complimentary tickets with prime seating to other events, such as sporting events. This usually consisted of two to four tickets, which it passed on to its client, who was then able to invite a select guest to join them for an unexpected treat. This event planning company excelled at making its customers look good to its customers. It made sure that it always placed that attribute at the top of *its* customer service list.

EMBRACE

Clients are looking for companies that embrace their business philosophy foibles and all, and that can offer them customer service to meet their needs without having to fully understand the reason why they may choose to do something. Sometimes it can be a matter of cultural differences, either national culture or corporate culture. One event planning company respected the fact that for one client, it was essential that a seemingly unending barrage of questions be answered on a moment's notice. It expected this as part of the client's customer service requirements. The client's national culture made it extremely important never to be placed in a position of losing face by not being able to answer a question. None of their senior executives ever wanted to go into a meeting with company officials unprepared to answer any question that could conceivably come up. A flurry of telephone calls by a number of executive committee members would take place before they were called into a meeting, and the same questions would be asked repeatedly.

Recognizing a pattern and knowing the reason why it was taking place allowed the event planning company to fully embrace cultural differences and look for ways to ease the client's anxiety as part of its commitment to customized service for its clients. Instead of waiting to be inundated by calls, the planners decided to take a proactive approach and devise a method whereby they could head off the questions in advance. The sales representative made it his mission to find out when the client's meetings were scheduled to take place and asked for a list of possible concerns from his main contact. The questions were given to the appropriate people in the event planning company to review, and an answer sheet was prepared and dispatched to all committee members. Sending it to only one would not have made the rest of the executive team feel at ease, because they all wanted to be prepared should they be called upon. His strategy to handle queries and client concerns was very successful and both sides were happy with the outcome.

One company owner and president talked a good game about staying on budget and managing his expenditures carefully, but his personal philosophy was quite different. Bluntly put, he did not want to fly economy or be transported to the hotel in the same mode of transportation that was being used for his guests. His personal preference was to fly first class, be transferred in top-of-the-line limousines and stay in one of the largest hotel suites, but he did not want to come out and say it. Every event would involve the same charade being played out. He would be booked on the same flights as his guests with no special concessions. It would be unthinkable for him to travel in first class on the same flights as his guests when they were sitting in coach. The tickets would be issued and the upgraded suite negotiated as part of the contract would be booked, although he did not get the presidential suite, which was his true heart's desire. The event planning company was unable to negotiate an upgrade on his air tickets, as his guests were flying in on a variety of aircraft and the quantity of purchased tickets per airline was not great enough for any one air carrier to offer the upgrade.

As the event moved closer, the client would look for excuses to fly in advance of the group, which would allow him to fly first class.

Then, he had to concoct a reason why someone else should have his suite and he would need another, much larger one to host cocktails in. Perhaps the presidential suite would work, or there was a private mansion located close by. Exactly what types of limousines were available at this location? This charade was the normal drill. To appease his conscience or uphold his company image the owner usually took the designated top sales winner with him on the first-class flight. This was the same person who had been upgraded to take his old suite, and at the end, it was said that this was a winning perk. This scenario was repeated several times until it finally clicked that what the client said he wanted done was not actually the case. He did not want the event planning company to search high and low for an alternate coach-class air seat to keep his budget in check.

This realization hit home when he booked a return overseas flight requiring an overnight stay en route so he could travel first class, when a direct flight that had only economy seats remaining was available. The event planning staff came up with a way to ensure the client got what he truly wanted and without having to come out and say it during committee meetings. They just embraced rather than questioned the way he as owner and company president chose to do business. Their intention was never to embarrass him, but in their quest for maintaining customer service and following his directive for budget management, they initially missed the message that he did not want helpful cost-saving suggestions regarding his personal travel put forward in front of his staff. Even though he was sitting in on meetings talking about the good time they, including himself, would have together flying as a group, he never truly intended to take part.

ENLIGHTEN

Customers look to their suppliers to enlighten them on ways to produce an event that will meet all of their objectives and do it more efficiently. They are counting on your company's expertise being made available to them as part of their customer service experience. Sometimes what they need to know is not directly related to the business at hand, but would hold future value to both of you in how they conduct their business. For example, a planner's experience working with a number of different clients and suppliers allows him to see how others conduct their business and offer suggestions that may help to ease workloads, such as using redline to mark tracked changes and apply strikethrough formatting to text or numbers in Word documents or contracts. It is more efficient and timesaving for all involved than deciphering revisions made by hand. There will be times the client will take your advice and other times that they will wish that they had. What is not acceptable in terms of customer service is seeing clients or their guests encounter areas of struggle and not stepping in with a workable solution. It is also not acceptable to let them knowingly breach protocol, cultural customs, business ethics or etiquette. If you know they could commit a faux pas by not having received proper instruction in advance, it is your responsibility as a planner to enlighten your clients. For example, how you tilt your wrist while pouring wine can be offensive in some countries, gestures common at home can be disrespectful in some parts of the world and even how you button your shirt or show the bottom of your shoe when seated can affront some nationalities.

One event planning company had a guest on a program who had very special medical needs. The event was taking place halfway around the world and she had to take her medicine at very specific times, with special food and other requirements. She expressed her concern and confusion about how to manage this while dealing with several time zones and not being in control of other key elements. The event planning company prepared a sheet that the client could take to her doctor that outlined her itinerary in great detail and noted all time changes, meal times, any physical demands, etc. To the event planning company, it was something it could easily prepare for the guest to take to her doctor to help put her mind at rest. To the client it was a major client service issue. Its guest had been enlightened with what she needed to know so that she could do the follow-up steps with her doctor. The client was pleased that his guests were being so well looked after and the incentive trip had not yet even begun.

An event planning staff member did his very best to enlighten his client on shipping dates for print material he wanted to have available during his meeting. The client was holding his annual meeting on a cruise ship and the event planning staff stressed the importance of making sure that any material being sent to the ship had to arrive by a specific date and ample time had to be allowed for customs clearance. If the boat set sail without the package arriving on time, it would be several days before he could hope to receive it, as the ship would be at sea and some of the ports of call did not have daily air service. The client ran late with preparing his material, and sending it by courier still would not ensure that it would reach the ship in time if the package was held up in customs. The planning company staff member recommended that key information be divided up among the client's staff to carry the material onboard with them in order to ensure the materials arrived at the boat on time. The client was dismissive of the staff member's suggestion. The package did not arrive on time and it was necessary to have the staff member stay behind to make arrangements to reroute it to the first major port of call. He then flew ahead to the destination so that he could assist in clearing it through customs on arrival and transfer it to the ship. The event planning company had done its best to enlighten its client about the possibilities but could not control his final actions. What it could do with regard to customer service was everything possible to make sure that the package was attended to and brought to the ship as early as it could be.

Government officials were coming to opening ceremonies at a very special event. This was a last-minute change and the client was thrilled to have such high-level dignitaries at her event. This was the first occasion of this sort for her and she had not been schooled in proper procedures and protocol. She depended on her event planning company's years of experience to tell her what must be done and how her staff should conduct themselves. The VIP guests' attendance had been totally unexpected and time required to ensure that proper etiquette was used had not been factored in, but came under the umbrella of customized customer service the event planning company provided for its clients. It would reflect poorly on both the event planning company and the client if anything was to go amiss. The planning company did not let her down and its knowledge of proper protocol saved the day.

EDUCATE

More and more customers are demanding educational advice in strategic planning, marketing, motivation, communication and public relations from their event planning companies as part of customer service. An event can be simply a means to an end, but done right, an event can be a valuable motivational or marketing tool that provides clients with an excellent return on their investment. Clients are looking for new techniques to enhance their business, help them operate more efficiently and produce better results. They trust their event planning company to keep to them updated as part of their customer service and look to them as an educational resource.

Technology is one educational area that comes up frequently. Clients are asking how best to incorporate the Web into upcoming events and programs to increase attendance and enhance the delegates' experience before, during and after each event. Often clients are not aware of the available options, such as Web surveys, personalized forms, detailed breakdowns on special preferences and accessibility requirements, as well as tools to send e-mail broadcasts (daily newsletter or updates) during each event. They look to their event planners to make recommendations and get their company up to speed. Today's planners must be educated and comfortable about the use of technology in order to stay in business and keep customers coming back year after year.

Clients also look to their event planning companies to educate them about their professional observances over the course of their event and to offer guidance where they may be misdirected, such as the type of event, inclusions or venue their guests enjoy.

One event planning company was concerned that the programs it was creating were not fully satisfying the needs of the guests, and although the client was thrilled with the results it knew it could make better choices for its client. This client was involved in direct sales marketing and she rewarded her top salespeople with upscale incentive programs. Her personal lifestyle was affluent and her hotel choices and locations reflected her individual preferences. Her winners came from small towns and rural areas and for many of them, their job was to help ends meet at home and provide a second income while being able to stay at home raising their families. The hotels they stayed in overwhelmed them, and many of them could not afford the prices at the resort. Most days only two meals were paid for by the company. Most of the guests could not afford to pick up the cost for the extra meals, as costs were extremely high at the resort, so they skipped meals that were not included in the program. Many of the lavish resorts they stayed at were not located close to less expensive meal options.

The event planning company witnessed a number of guests slipping extra fruit, rolls and yogurts from their breakfast buffet into their bags as a means to tide them over until dinner. They knew the reason why. A number of guests had mentioned the high prices to the event planning staff. The budget was already pushed to the maximum and the client was unwilling to reduce the number of days on program so that the money saved could be put into providing three meals a day for guests. The event planning company proposed a compromise—an upscale all-inclusive resort where all meals, beverages, activities, sightseeing entertainment and tipping was included. The response of the guests to the next incentive program was amazing—the numbers doubled. The event planning company had discovered something important. In the past, some salespeople preferred to take a lesser prize because they could not afford the cost of meals not provided for by the company or the expense of expected formal attire they would never use in their day-to-day lives. Moving the incentive to a resort where they would incur no additional expenses put their minds at rest and they were overjoyed to be able to now take part. It was the event planning company's role to educate its client on what would hold appeal and motivate its guests. The company president had to put aside her personal preferences in order to do what was right for her staff and her company. Staying at upscale luxury resorts was best left to her personal travel and not part of her company's incentive programs.

ENRICH

Every client expects to come away from their event having learned something that will help their company go and grow forward. They know they are working with a creative industry that is skilled in motivational techniques and operational expertise and hope to take away something from the experience they can use in the future, enriching the events they plan by making them more meaningful and rewarding. This is an added value service that event planning companies can provide that will enhance working relationships.

One event planning company convinced its client to try taking its business meeting out of a ballroom, where it typically held its functions, and do something fun to launch its new product line. The event planning company felt that the format its client was using was growing stale. The client was a candy manufacturer and the event planning company proposed taking over a movie theater complex to launch its latest confectionery line. The marquee was changed to the client's company logo and the concession bar featured its newest offering. The setting was perfect for doing the presentation, launching its newest commercial and then enjoying a private showing of a feature film. For the employees, the venue was unexpected, festive and fun in keeping with the new candy product, which would be available for sale at movie theaters, and had the office buzzing the next day. The cost of holding the event at the movie theater was actually lower than the regular meeting. With the next product launch the client was very open to looking at new venues and never went back to doing its launches in a ballroom. The reaction it received by doing something new was rewarding to not only the client but the event planning company as well.

One event planner honed her budget projection skills in her attempt to meet her client's customer service expectations in preparing its budget. She became so adept at calculating costs that she was constantly on or under budget, even on multi-million-dollar programs. The executive in charge of the client's program was thrilled with her results. Her accuracy enhanced his reputation for money management, as there were never any surprises at final reconciliation. This ability—driven by customer service—gave her company a tremendous advantage over its competition. The company knew that its client prized fiscal responsibility highly and that was what the event planning company had said was one of its top commitments to its clients. In the past, the client had worked with an event planning company that had underestimated its program costs by 20 percent or more by inaccurate price "estimates." The client's representatives, wary of working with someone new, braced themselves for unexpected expenses showing up at final reconciliation. They were delighted when costs came in as projected, and were very vocal to others in their industry about the level of customer service they had received—which led to business referrals.

ENERGIZE

Companies are looking to their event planning company not only to motivate their sales staff and guests but to energize and invigorate their internal staff as well. It can be difficult to motivate staff who will not be attending the event. To them, it is simply an added task and they are saddled with such frustrating choices as chasing their invitees for answers. They have no personal stake in the event and require the expertise of the event planning staff to steward them through the logistics and have them exhilarated about the vital role they are playing in their company's success. In some instances, the event planner may have no direct interaction with the guests until the actual event and they have to depend on the client's frontline staff to properly set the mood of anticipation that is critical to the event's success. If they make disparaging remarks to participants about the program or give away too much information, such as some of the surprise event elements, motivation can be lost. For example, one company was flying in top-name entertainment and wanted to heighten anticipation by not revealing who until they walked out on stage. Had staff divulged who was flying in, the emotion of delight they were hoping to evoke would have been lessened. Part of customer service imparted by event planning companies is the ability to make everyone feel good about what is being achieved, the valuable role they play and to convey a sense of responsibility for their company achieving its objectives.

One event planning company does this by making sure that those it has worked with share in the excitement of a job well done by letting them know how valuable their role is to the success of the program. The planners take the time to explain why something has to be done a certain way instead of making endless demands without any explanation. They are aware that there can be a feeling of letdown that follows the final push and they know the value of sending a pick-me-up. They make sure that a creative thank-you gift—that the office can share in—arrives in their office on the day of the event, thanking them for their help, and along the way send out inexpensive thank yous that let others know that what they are doing is essential to the event. A novel thank you was a bag filled to the brim with Lifesavers, thanking them for being a lifesaver in meeting a time-sensitive deadline.

EXCITE

An important part of customer service is feeling genuine excitement for the client's event. For example, you may have designed countless team-building events over the years but the client's staff haven't. They want to feel excited about what they are doing and look for support and assurance from the event planning staff. If the event planning staff are blasé, the client's staff may start to question whether or not their guests will be eager to take part in what they believe is a great idea. They may start to second-guess their decision and could end up requiring constant reassurances that what they are doing will work. If the event planning staff are excited about what they have created, it will spill over to the guests, suppliers and the client's internal staff, and that feeling only enhances the actual event experience.

Excitement creates event energy, something event planning companies and their customers strive for. Excitement is not limited to the day of the event. It starts to build from the moment planning begins and continues through event operations to on-site orchestration. The final moments before everyone begins to arrive and everything is in its place can be magical and the feeling should be savored. Once the event kicks in it is sometimes difficult to pause for a moment to take everything in as it swirls around you. But making a moment to let the event energy run through you and touch all your senses should be mandatory because that is what event planning is all about.

One event planner was brokenhearted to have to remain behind due to pneumonia and not get to see a very special event she had created come to fruition. If she physically could have walked to the plane, she would have. Watching the look in the guests' eyes when they walked into a room—in this case it was a beautiful ocean view setting—and seeing what was in store for them meant everything to her and helped fuel her excitement for the next event she created. Her excitement in the days leading up to the event was contagious, and while guests did not know what to expect they were anticipating a night to remember. That is what they got. Some customers talk about service with a smile, but customer service offered with excitement takes you so much further.

To see the effect a lack of excitement has on an event, you only have to look back to the planning of the world's biggest party—the millennium. Special event planning took a downturn because of all the gloom-and-doom predictions. People were afraid to fly or even go out because Y2K glitches were supposed to disrupt things like electricity. Widespread chaos was expected. People were storing water, candles and food instead of planning a celebration. A once-in-a-lifetime event was diminished due to a lack of excitement, and that can happen to events of any size.

ENVIRONMENT

Customers are looking for a safe event planning company environment in which to place their event. They want the conditions at the event planning company to mirror their own company's work ethics and corporate culture. They want to work with people who value their business and show respect for their event. They expect as part of customer service that client confidentiality will be top of the list. Lack of discretion on behalf of some event planning companies and their suppliers has led to some companies insisting on nondisclosure clauses being added to their contracts, requiring everyone who is working on their account and on the day of event (e.g., waitstaff) to sign confidentiality agreements with severe financial repercussions if trust is broken. While companies may do business with event planning companies who handle others in their industry, they want to make sure that what they are doing is not shared with others and that no tales will be told of on-site high spirits. Trust is a very important customer service element and once broken is difficult to repair; there is a sense of betrayal that is not easily undone. Customers do not want to hear war stories about other clients because if they do their trust will be shaken. If an event planning company will talk about other companies they do business with, clients know that they may be next on the list. And they don't want to hear staff speaking disrespectfully to one another or about each other.

Customers want a safe environment in which to place their money, as well as their trust. They expect companies to be as mindful of their money as they are with their own and will be unforgiving of waste. They know that their jobs can be on the line if their trust in their event planning company is unfounded.

One company was very impressed by its event planning company's creativity and business acumen. The client's company name had the power to make others drool with anticipation of the event planning dollars that could be spent. The event planning company that won its account, however, dazzled the decision-makers with its innovative ideas that cost half of what they were expecting to pay. It knew that it had found a safe environment in which to place its trust and money. What the planner proposed was something new and fresh that had amazing tie-in potential for the theme event. For the event planner it was not about the dollars the client had to spend; it was about finding exactly the right venue for its event. It would have been simpler to design an event that matched the client's objectives in a hotel ballroom and in doing so spend a fortune on decor, which was what the client was expecting. Had the event planning company taken this more traditional route it would have made substantially more money, but that was not its objective. What mattered most was creating a stand-out event that would have the media buzzing and guests raving. And that is exactly what transpired. The planner found a perfect restaurant venue that required very little in the way of decor enhancements, as it was over the top and fit the evening's theme. The drawback was that the venue had never closed to the public before—and was apprehensive about what would be required to handle 1,500 people arriving at once, but it was an added bonus for the client as it became the first company to hold an exclusive event there. The event planner's expertise put the restaurant's owners at ease and they consented to having the event. The logistics were intricate but well worth the effort. At three in the morning, the client's guests showed no sign of departing. They were lingering, reluctant to end such a memorable occasion.

How the event planner presented his theme option helped him capture the client's attention. His creativity extended to his proposal. It was very easy to see from his presentation that finding a creative approach to meeting the client's objectives was the main focus of this event planning company, not the amount of money he could possibly make off of the client. The client knew it had found a company whose work ethics and environment reflected its own.

Work to create an environment that enables your business to achieve customer service goals.

EMPLOYEES

Companies are spending a great deal of money these days trying to ensure that they find exactly the right employee, one who can meet their customers' needs. They are posting their job opportunities in industry publications, on association websites or paying employees referral fees for helping them find the right fit for the company. They feel they will attract qualified employees if they target where they post their ads and will get better results than listing an opening in the local newspaper. Some event planning companies are turning to industry headhunters to judge the worth of potential candidates before meeting with them or to entice sought-after individuals to consider working for them. And headhunting executives are employing professional companies to conduct in-depth reference reviews and provide them with an evaluation. Staff considerations are then put through personality, intelligence and aptitude tests, as well as handwriting assessments, which can analyze character traits.

Companies know the liability of making the wrong hire. It can cost them untold headaches and hard costs and even business and customers. They also know the value of having a stable environment with long-term employees who come to know their customers' likes and dislikes and are capable of growing with them to meet their changing needs. Event planning companies are faced with requiring specific skills to run their business, and staff turnover can be a problem. Clients get anxious when their files are turned over to new staff members; they fear that something important may go overlooked. When customers see names and faces changing rapidly in a company, it sends out a signal that they should be concerned.

Top employers work hard to make sure that there is little room for communication breakdown between their staff and their customers. They work on creating strategies that will eliminate customer service frustrations and make sure that both their staff and their clients receive what they each need to nurture good working relationships and uphold company values.

Clients appreciate when staff connect with and care about their guests. One customer was very impressed with an employee's attention to its guest's travel needs. She recommended an overnight stay for one of its top producers on his return flight so that he would not arrive at his final destination too late. The participant lived in an isolated area where there was a problem with moose on the road, making night driving dangerous. He was very apprehensive about arriving back at night, and the employee noted his concern. She also made similar recommendations for several of the other guests, ones that would put the client in a very good light with its employees, and found ways to do it that were cost efficient. That in turn made her company look good. She saw a need, followed her company's criteria for customer service, which was customer satisfaction, and found a solution that worked for everyone involved.

Top event planning employees often find themselves listed by name in client proposals. They become an indispensable marketing tool that companies can actively promote to their clients. Highly skilled event planning employees that have made a name for themselves in the industry are a valuable asset and can help their company attract new business and maintain clients.

EFFICIENCY

It is important to find out if your proposed plan for efficient customer service fits into your client's requirements. When you are dealing with day-to-day deadlines and event logistics you are dealing not with the company but an individual. The executives who have contracted the event are not the ones handling the frontline requests from the event planning company and the person who is assigned to manage the file internally may not have been part of the decision-making process and may need time to be familiarized with the event. For an event planning company, event planning is its business, but for the client it is only a small part in its daily activities. Planners need to keep in mind that the person assigned by the company to oversee the event plans also has his or her own work responsibilities and timelines to meet. The person may be seasoned in the role as the liaison between the company and the event planning company, or may be a novice taking on a new company project. It is important to find out the person's level of experience, workload, expectations and style of doing business. Both companies have a responsibility to manage their business as well as the event. It aids in customer relationships if the event planning company can create a critical path document to prepare the client's representative as to what will be coming, and acquaint them with what will be required from them and by when in order for the planner to execute a successful event. If they know in advance what to expect it can aid them in planning their time so that they can be more efficient. It is important that the event planning company carefully review its requirements with its client and make it aware of any financial or other event repercussions that could occur if payment schedules, attrition, cancellation, printing, ticketing, room list, and food and beverage guarantee dates are not adhered to. The event planning company and the client also need to sit down and discuss times when key people will be out of the office and adjust the critical path accordingly. Doing this exercise together will also alert you to crunch time periods and red flag areas.

Two top company executives went on vacation at the same time, leaving no one in charge to make critical decisions that would have a financial impact on their program. A review of business and travel plans early could have allowed planning to accommodate for such things. Normally there would have been no problem with the two executives being away at the same time, as their job duties did not overlap, but in this case they were the two top decision-makers responsible for the internal budget management of their event. It gave the appearance of inefficiency when their vacations had to be interrupted so that the program could move forward. Another company's signing officer was away on business and left her company without checks to pay the company's suppliers, which put certain event elements at risk. Had she been advised in advance to expect a check request, provisions could have been made.

Plan out how to work together efficiently and effectively. Find out what time of day is best to be in touch and what method of correspondence is preferred. One planner and her client liaison discovered that they were both in the office by 7:00 a.m., so they arranged "breakfast meetings" over the telephone. The planner prepared a recap of any outstanding matters or authorized changes that required customer sign-off, and sent them over to the client in writing later in the day. The client's representative could then proceed with her regular workday and follow up with her participants at a time that worked best for her. At the end of her day, she would take a few moments before heading home to pull together what she would need for the next morning's review. The client's representative liked conferring each day, as she wanted to be fully prepared should her boss require an update.

Finding the best method to work efficiently, meshing together two different working styles and providing customized service does not mean that it is acceptable to abuse staff or allow another company to jeopardize your business. Some clients, caught up in the excitement, act as though they are the only client that an event planning company is servicing and can make excessive demands or ride roughshod on staff who they feel are not living up to their unreasonable expectations. Event planning companies still need to manage their business as well as their events, and sometimes this involves managing their clients so that they both can work more productively.

One event planning company was plunged into turmoil every time a client called, and that was several times a day. If his calls were not returned within minutes he had the tendency to simply show up in its office, located nearby. In the beginning, staff were startled to look up and see him striding through the door without having given them a moment to act on his request. He had the tendency to make himself familiar in the office, pouring himself a coffee and then sitting down at a desk wanting to chitchat, while interrupting precious workday moments. Sometimes there are pressing time restraints and limited hours in which event planning staff can reach their suppliers, and an unexpected visit can play havoc on deadlines. This is especially true for event planning companies that do international events and are constantly juggling their work around time zones. The staff did not have a buffer. The situation grew intolerable as the visits escalated up to several times a day and appropriate action had to be taken by the sales representative and company owner. Customer service is a two-way street; it is not just about what customers require from you but also what you as a planner require from them in order to operate their program and service them efficiently. In this case the onus was put on the sales representative to manage his client and clearly establish the ground rules that would enable his client and his office to work together in harmony without either feeling abused or neglected.

EVALUATE

While most event planning companies conduct event evaluations and reconciliation reviews with staff members, suppliers and client, seldom is an evaluation that is customer service specific carried out. Many companies operate under the assumption if there are no complaints, customers are satisfied, although this is not necessarily the case. Often a customer's seeds of discontent can grow without coming to the attention of its event planning company, and the same applies between event planning companies and their suppliers. It is sometimes easier to look for a new supplier than to delve into what is making them unhappy from a customer service standpoint. The event may have been a success but if day-to-day dealings were too unpleasant or not up the standards the client expected, the client will look for someone with a similar product or service with whom it may be able to develop a working relationship that better fits its needs. As the client and planner work through the event planning and operations stages they can identify their company working styles and what is working and what is missing. If they proceed to a second event together, they both know where they need to make adjustments. To some clients the effort may not be worthwhile and they move on without ever talking about what was troubling them. This may occur because they believe that change in the direction they require is not possible or probable.

One client, tired of his staff's complaints about the event planning company's receptionist and accounting staff's brusque manner and demeaning attitude to them, simply chose not to do business with them again. He gave his sales representative a song and dance about why they were not doing any more events at this time. The client attributed the internal staff's bad behavior to the event planning company's corporate culture. To the client, obviously it was acceptable behavior in the event planning company, as it was not being addressed and dealt with by the company owners, and the employees with the questionable conduct had been with the event planning company for years. It was affecting more than one service area in his company and he did not want the event planning company's bad attitude spreading into his company by appearing to condone it. He had been pleased with the event planning company's sales representative, and when she moved to another company he opened the door for her to bid again and finally voiced his past concerns. Remember that once an event has been contracted, it becomes the office's, not just the sales representative's, responsibility to properly service the client. If the event planning staff display a lack of professionalism in their day-to-day interactions with the client's staff members, it can cost a company future business.

Some companies, concerned about customer service levels, conduct exit interviews and evaluations with clients whose business they have lost, as well as ongoing evaluations with existing clients. They know the expense that goes into acquiring new clients and if there is something they could possibly do to bring about change and in the process retain a client, they are willing to look at how working relationships could be improved between their two companies. These companies, seeking to do better and grow their business, are looking for ways to give themselves a competitive edge in customer service by understanding what each one of their clients need and expect from them, and they are not afraid to take an objective look at where they could improve.

ETHICS AND ETIQUETTE

Two important qualities that lead to excellence in customer service are business ethics and etiquette. Personal and professional business ethics must be of the highest standards and staff should be masters of business etiquette. Company codes of conduct must be established, and it is imperative to review with staff their expected behavior both in and out of the office. *Event Planning: Ethics and Etiquette: A Principled Approach to the Business of Special Event Management* (John Wiley & Sons, 2003) offers guidelines for establishing ethical policies in the office and on site at events with clients and their guests. It offers techniques to keep personal and professional boundaries from being crossed. Event planners on the front line dealing with clients and their guests often find themselves in situations in which they need a professional code, a guide to dealing with tricky questions of ethics or etiquette. They know that with a thoughtless act or a less-than-tactful word, long-lasting business relationships can be ruined forever. At times they can feel as though they are navigating a minefield of potentially sticky situations that can easily blow up in their face. In order to circumvent this from happening and to reach an excellent standard of service, companies must be prepared to invest the time and the money to fully train their staff in the areas of business ethics and etiquette.

It is important to put practices in place that will enable your company to move forward and grow with your clients. Not keeping pace with your clients (and your competitors) and not evolving with them is consequential—if you don't change with your customers or lead the way, you can easily find them slipping away.

Stating that you offer excellent customer service in your proposal or presentation means nothing to clients. It is a phrase clients hear every day from everyone who is soliciting their business. Meaning can be given to this expression by demonstrating understanding of the client's industry and their company's industry-related requirements. In your proposal or presentation, outline exactly how your company can offer superior customer service that has been tailored specifically to fit the client. Doing so will set you apart from competition that merely includes listing it as one of its features. Offering customized service can be a valuable marketing tool.

Before you can offer customers customized customer service, it is essential that your company standards have been established. Office dress, demeanor, procedures and codes of conduct must be firmly in place. These will provide the foundation for strong customer service standards and work ethics to be built on. Only once these are firmly in place can you begin to determine each individual client's expectations of how they would like their account serviced.

Questions to ask to help determine your client's customer service requirements include:

- How can we best service you?

- Does your industry have any special needs on site we should be aware of?

- What would you ideally like to receive from us in the way of customer service?

- What is important to you in terms of service?

- Do you prefer us to contact you by e-mail, fax, over the telephone or in person, for example, in weekly meetings?

- Is there a time of day that works best for you?

- Who will we be working with to finalize event details?

- What specific areas will they be responsible for?

- What support will they need us from us in order for us both to work efficiently and effectively?

- Are there any reports that you require from us on an ongoing basis, such as budget updates?

- Do you prefer your reports to be in the form of an executive summary or of a detailed report?

- Are there any special considerations that we should take into account?

- Are there any in-house systems we need to be aware of, such as the schedule for your intercompany mail if guest information is being sent out internally?

- When do you require invoices from us to meet your check runs and payment schedule dates?

- When are your peak periods?

- When is your year-end? Is there anything you will require from us at that time?

- Who will have final sign-off authority and approval to request changes?

- Do you know when key people will be out of the office on business or travel so that we can make sure that we have everything we need from them?

- How would you like us to handle special requests from your participants?

- How much event information do you want us to share with your participants?

- How would you prefer us to address your participants?

- Are there any special services we could provide that would be of value to you, such as training?

PART 3

Marketing Endeavors

These days it seems that everywhere we turn, someone is trying to get our attention, and at times it seems there is no escape from the seemingly endless flow of e-mails filling up our inboxes, the flood of mail that comes across our desks or through our post boxes at home, and the incessant flashing message alert on our telephones. We are barraged by television commercials, and the shows themselves seem to get shorter. During sweeps week or high-profile shows such as the televised Super Bowl, where advertisers pay a premium price to advertise, it sometimes feels like they are squeezing a little entertainment between the commercials. Advertisers know people are using VCRs to fast-forward through their commercials or TIVO looking to ignore them entirely, so they are now turning to using product placement within shows to counter this consumer maneuver. Going to the movies used to offer a way of escape, but today movies have actual commercials along with movie trailers, which are actually commercials themselves.

Some movie patrons were so incensed when they showed up on time for a film but had to sit through 15 minutes of advertising that they demanded a refund and that movie theaters start posting both the advance seating time and the movie start time. Magazines are heavier than ever, so filled with ads that you feel as though you are turning pages forever before you come to a story. They are also brimming with mail-in offer cards for subscriptions, no longer attached firmly to the magazine but blown into the magazine pages, building irritation as opposed to desire as they flutter to the floor. Television, movies and magazines have all banded together, and now you will find ads within the ads with both subtle and shameless product placement—consumer goods in film and television—that leave you wondering exactly how many times they can work the advertiser's name or product into the show. In the past, viewers rarely saw product names, for example, on cans of beverages, boxes of cereal or clothing, but now that advertisers are paying for the rights to have their product displayed, characters are shown holding or wearing easily identifiable brands, mentioning the product by name or putting the product on a counter.

Specialty lighting has now been developed that lets advertisers place ads on the actual walls of subway tunnels where before there was only darkness, and subway advertisers are not stopping with visual effects. In Europe, singing ads, marketing products, have now been launched.

"Can you hear me now?" is the refrain of a cell phone company and the cry of advertisers as they vie for your attention and your spending dollars. When U.S. citizens were given the option of being placed on a Do Not Call Registry to eliminate telephone solicitation from telemarketers, more than 51 million people signed up. Their message was loud and clear. They were tired of being bombarded with people trying to sell them something. Finally the public had a way of saying to advertisers, "Can you hear *us* now?"

And CNN reported that the Federal Communications Commission approved a US$5.4 million fine against a company for sending unsolicited advertisements to consumers and violating their 1992 "do not fax" rule. Consumers have had enough of being inundated with what they consider to be resource-wasting junk mail.

This is what sales representatives are up against every day as they set out to win new accounts for their company. To potential clients they are being cold called; just another voice clamoring to be heard, a person who will eat up valuable time from their day, take them away from their work and possibly even force them to stay late to finish an assignment they ran behind on due to answering unsolicited calls. To them, you are the time enemy that must be waylaid at any cost, unless they can see immediate value in talking to you, reading your proposal or meeting you face to face. If you don't capture their attention in the first 20 seconds, your calls won't be returned, your e-mail entreats will be deleted as spam and your introduction letter be filed in the "circular file."

Part Three of this book deals with marketing endeavors. Chapter 7 covers how to market to your audience to increase a positive response. With only 20 seconds for your marketing message to resonate with clients, how you lead in is of utmost importance, and fresh new ways that have had proven success will be outlined.

Chapter 8 reviews innovative ways to solicit sales. If creativity is part of what you are selling, it has to be demonstrated in what you say, send and do when first making contact with your potential client.

In Chapter 9, the value of diversifying is discussed. Event planners have experienced how quickly business can disappear, and know that selling to only one type of client can be damaging, jeopardizing their very existence, if something major occurs in their industry.

One of the biggest marketing endeavors that both experienced and entrepreneurial, fresh out-of-university-or-college event planning grads will face is how to promote themselves and their businesses when they make the decision to go out on their own. Chapter 10 examines some of the considerations to take into account when you begin to look at when, or whether or not, you should open your own event planning business.

7
MARKETING TO YOUR AUDIENCE

Event planning companies and their suppliers are masters in the art of creating events that inspire, motivate, dazzle and delight clients and their guests. However, seldom are the same skills and principles they know so well and use every day applied to their client introduction letters, presentation kits, promotional material or websites. Many display an appalling lack of ingenuity and imagination for an industry that prides itself on being innovative. When the product you are selling is your company as a creative resource, offering solutions to meet special needs through the medium of events, everything you do and put forth should be reflective of the statement you are making. If your letter of introduction and brochure say ho hum, what is that saying to the client about your other imaginative concepts? When the world is vying for your customers' attention it is important to devise a way in which to stand out from the crowd, not only in the events that you do but also in the manner in which you present yourself.

Your marketing endeavors should pack a powerful punch that displays your inventiveness and be as effective as the events you produce. The message you are conveying about yourself, your product and your company should be consistent regardless of the marketing vehicle you are using, and in order to make an impact it must have four key elements when you launch your campaign.

The four key elements of a marketing campaign are:

- Lots of Energy
- A Platform
- A Strong Hook
- Sharp Focus

LOTS OF ENERGY

Event planners strive to make sure that every event they plan has energy, that the event elements they include produce an event that is upbeat, unusual or interesting and that nothing falls flat so that the participants leave feeling energized. They do it as a matter of course when they are envisioning an event, choosing the exact date that will capture maximum attendance, considering possible locations and assessing the pros and cons, selecting the venue, making sure that the room is the right fit for the group size and looking at which room lay-out works best and deciding on the event elements that will meet their clients' objectives. They strive to eliminate dead air, dead space, congestion and anything that will detract or take away energy from their program. Planners know how to structure an event so that there are no time lags, people standing around bored, or dead air, which occurs when there is no life or energy taking place in the room. They look for venues that fit the size of the group so that they do not encounter dead space, the result of energy getting lost in a space that is too big. They seek to avoid areas of congestion, long lineups and unnecessary delays because they know how quickly guests can become disgruntled, frustrated and annoyed with any inconvenience they experience due to poor strategic planning. There is a successful formula for creating an event with energy and planners simply adapt it to fit their clients.

Event planning companies manage clients from many industries and there is variation even in a single industry. An event planning company that specializes in handling corporate functions will still have a client base that is very mixed. For example, one company could have clients that are in the financial, pharmaceutical, automotive, real estate, confectionery, widget manufacturing and entertainment industries. And companies planning events for the social sector may coordinate weddings, society events, nonprofit charity events, fashion shows, gala fundraisers, sporting events, festivals, musical soirees, balls, parties and premieres. Some event planning companies do both corporate and social events and juggle the different demands of both with ease. No matter what sort of event they are doing, planners working on corporate or social events are accustomed to creating events and marketing them to their clients' guests in a manner that will speak to them, capture their attention and create anticipation. The teaser campaign, print material and actual event that they would plan for a client in the financial industry would be very different from the one they would design for an entertainment company. Both would have lots of energy but it would be energy created to target a specific market to elicit explicit responses and emotions. An event for the entertainment industry would be edgier than one for a financial company. For example, one event for the entertainment community included scantily dressed go-go dancers in cages, which was a huge success and very apropos. Meanwhile, a private event for a more conservative corporate client was held in a strip club and featured pole dancers, and was deemed unfitting by the company president, who was unaware of the venue choice and event entertainment elements. He fired the head of his event committee to appease his clients who had attended the event and were shocked by its inappropriateness. Though the entertainment event pushed certain boundaries that would not be appropriate or deemed proper in financial circles, both industries share a desire to produce events that set trends and get people talking. For example, what takes place at the music awards geared to a younger crowd in terms of dress, stage acts, decor and entertainment would not be acceptable at a more conservative event such as the Oscars. The same principle would apply if you were handling a wedding or a movie premiere. These are both social events, but they are two very different clients with very different needs to be addressed. A wedding is steeped in emotion, tradition and romance, while a movie premiere seeks splash and media attention.

In many event planning offices, sales representative are busy sending letters of introduction and promotional material out to a myriad of potential customers from all industries. In many cases, sales representatives have several form letters that they use. They simply adapt the boilerplate and incorporate any pertinent information, and send one out with a sales kit hoping to wow the client and open the door for a meeting. One sales representative would provide his receptionist with a potential client's vital information and request the "ABC Soup" or "XYZ Company" letter be used, and off it would be sent with no further thought to whether or not the style of the letter or the content actually spoke to the recipient in their industry language and conveyed energy, excitement and enticement. The language that speaks to a financial institution and may serve to get its attention and get it excited could be based on facts and figures, while an entertainment company's might be visual—but that is not always the case. Each company, just as each event does, needs to be thoroughly researched.

If you can convey to companies that an incentive program you designed was so successful that it was necessary to do the event back to back over the course of three weeks, or that response from sales staff was so incredible that you sold out an entire hotel, that will convey energy to them and get them excited about the possibility of working with someone who could produce such outstanding results. You will have hit their hot button and will have created an impression. If you simply send a letter that holds no substance and essentially says nothing more than "enclosed please find a company kit and we hope to have the opportunity to do business with you," you will have lost them at the start. Focus must be paid not only to what is being said and seen but how the marketing message is delivered to the client. Does it show an instant understanding of their industry and their distinctive needs, get your audience's attention and hit a nerve by communicating energy?

A PLATFORM

A platform is a declaration of the principles upon which your company proposes to stand. This can be incorporated into your marketing plans and become a platform from which to launch your promotional campaign. What is the message you are trying to put across to clients and to the public? What foundation are you using to launch your personal and professional marketing and publicity campaign? What beliefs and principles are you putting forward?

These are topics that need to be reviewed and established before the sales and marketing process begins.

If a company skips this vital step and allows sales staff to run rampant, each member of the sales force can conceivably be sending out a different message to clients, one that fits his or her own agenda and not necessarily the company's. Sales representatives are selling not only the company they work for but themselves as well. If they and the company they are presently working for ever part ways, sales representatives are hopeful that their relationship with the client is so strong that they will follow them to the new company. Of course, the planning company is aspiring to retain the client itself. Sales representatives know that their professional reputation can be enhanced or diminished by the company they choose to represent, just as they themselves can bring added credibility or prove to be a liability to the company they work for.

It is in both parties' interests—the company's and the sales force's—to make sure that the platforms they are launching their marketing efforts from are compatible, and that great care is given to the message they both bring to potential clients and the manner in which it is being put forth. For example, if the company's platform is to provide quality service to a select clientele and the sales reps are intent on signing up anyone that crosses their path, their marketing and business direction is not in sync.

One hotel marketing company whose platform was representing a specific level of hotel that met the needs of a very select clientele was dismayed when it received the sales kit of a particular hotel. While the property itself was outstanding, this was in no way conveyed by its promotional material. In order for it to be able to successfully market the product to its clients, the marketing company knew that it had to have the hotel totally revamp its brochures. The hotel representative had a proven history of producing millions of dollars in revenue for the hotels she represented and she did not want her company's reputation damaged by sending out a sales kit that was below standard. Both the hotel and the representative had the same platform and they were a good fit, but the way in which the hotel was presenting itself in its marketing material was not. With a few necessary changes, the brochure was brought up to par, truly reflecting the property with a more fitting look that stood out visually and delivered the hotel's message to its targeted audience. Both parties went on to enjoy a very profitable working relationship.

A STRONG HOOK

When faced with only 20 seconds to grab someone's attention, developing a strong hook to pull in the audience and make them want to know more is a marketing must. This applies equally to your approach whether you are speaking to someone on the telephone during a cold call, sending literature out in the mail hoping to garner attention, setting up a website, running an ad, sending an e-mail or doing any other promotional activity.

Many people give only a casual glance to material that crosses their desk before deciding whether to read on, file it for future reference or discard it. Think about how fast your finger hits the delete or block sender key when an unsolicited e-mail comes in that doesn't immediately capture your attention. Consider how you flip through newspapers and magazines and change radio stations, and how you view television with one hand on the remote to quickly change channels. But suddenly something, a word, a song, an image captures your attention and your imagination. The moment when you pause is when you have been hooked to learn more, hear more, see more, explore more. That flash when the targeted audience is hooked is what you want to create in your marketing. Once hooked, people are in the position of wanting to know more.

A hook is not limited to something said verbally or expressed by the written word. It can also apply to something that you touch, see, feel, hear or smell. Some companies are now making sure that the music clients hear when they are placed on hold is no longer filler Musak but fitted to the company's image. The same applies to background music that is played in the office—matching music to the architecture of the office or the feeling desired and in the process building layers onto the company's brand identity. These companies know the value of marketing to the senses.

A festival looking for a new marketing idea decided to use another sense and added the sweet smell of success to its campaign. The dates and activities for its apple festival was being promoted in a telephone directory and the staff wanted to do something different to attract attention. They introduced the scent of apples to their ad, hoping to entice people to come to their event by stimulating their senses and bringing back memories. They hoped that the smell of fresh apples would hook potential visitors into reading further and discovering more about their festival. Their marketing campaign was very successful and it received media play as well, which was an unexpected bonus. This concept, one planners already use at events by adding sensory special effects, can be used in marketing ventures too.

Many event planning companies use the hook to great success creating events but neglect to adapt and apply the same knowledge to their sales and marketing endeavors. Good event planners use the hook technique when they are preparing teaser campaigns and invitations. They know that the right hook can set the tone for their event, excite people to attend and create allure. Planners know that the quality of the paper they use to produce their print material is important. They carefully choose colors, fonts and adornments. They take size and layout into consideration. They weigh the options of having the envelope handwritten for a more personalized touch than a more formal printed one. They even care about the stamp, the packaging and the delivery. Good event planners also use the hook when designing their events. They pull out all stops to market to the senses and pull people in. The same principles used by event planning companies in their design process can easily translate into creating a more marketable client approach, one with a definite hook that will give their company a competitive edge right from the start. Hit every possible hook as hard as possible but take care not to mix them up and muddy the message.

SHARP FOCUS

Just as some sales representatives use the shotgun approach to solicit sales, some companies do that with their marketing pieces. They throw everything in and end up creating a poor impression by not having a sharp focus, one that is targeted to a particular client, industry or need. They fail to match the interest of their potential customers with their abilities, and simply send the same presentation out to everyone. If companies and their sales reps do not conduct basic research and avail themselves of information that is easily accessible, they are setting themselves up to fail.

There are more chances for success and attracting interest if more time is spent sending out effective proposals that have strong individual client focus. Time spent analyzing a client's needs, their event criteria and their interests is not wasted. A company introductory letter should address potential clients about how their needs will be met and how there is a match, and it should be unique in that the message is tailored to them and not simply a form letter. If you want to stimulate interest in your company, your approach must bring forth that emotion.

When care is taken to develop your client list and your presentation with a sharp focus, you will find that it is easy to identify a client that is not a match for your service and that may not fit your criteria for what you are looking for in a client. It may not have an appropriate budget to do the type of event that is best suited to your company, or you may not be the best fit for helping it to reach its objective. It may have a reputation of being a difficult client, perhaps one that doesn't pay on time, is always nickeling and diming its suppliers and makes impossible demands, such as one client that want all cancellation charges to be waived right up to the day of the actual event, which is unreasonable as suppliers would have to pay their suppliers for food, beverage and services purchased on the client's behalf that close to an event.

If you define your focus and refine your client list to ensure a fit, then you end up not wasting your time or your target's. You need to bring objectivity into the exercise. You may also find clients you would like to work with but whose needs you are not yet qualified to fill. Being able to identify your next steps to take in order to acquire this account is a valuable marketing exercise. It shows you where you have to focus your energies and where you have to grow.

MARKETING OPPORTUNITIES

Event planning companies market themselves to new and existing customers in a variety of ways. They hope to elicit interaction in four main ways.

- In Their Offices
- At Industry Functions
- Where They Play Socially
- Created Opportunities

In Their Offices

Traditional ways that event planning companies, suppliers and their sales representatives reach potential clients in the office are by telephone, via e-mail, by mail, in person during sales calls and through their websites.

Trying to reach possible customers by telephone can be daunting at times, as many of the decision-makers are senior executives and they most likely have assistants running interference for them. Until you can convince them of the value you can bring to their company, they will simply dismiss you as an interruption or even a threat to their getting work done. Most people today are fending off numerous telephone calls in addition to sorting through a mountain of uninvited mail and e-mail messages. The sales representative usually tries to create rapport with her potential client's assistant, and if she cannot speak directly to her actual targets she tries to leave detailed messages or at least send her material in to the assistants, making sure that it is visibly marked "as requested."

If that sales maneuver fails, hoping to catch their potential client's assistant at lunch or the client in an unguarded moment early or late in the day when most people aren't in the office, some reps will key in specialty numbers that block caller I.D. in the hopes that their call will go through without showing their company name and alerting the client that it is a sales rep calling. They are anticipating the client will pick up in person or they will be able to leave a voice mail on their direct line. Those initial 20 seconds when they reach the assistant, the customer or the message machine are critical and should not be left to chance. There are only seconds to make an impression and not have your message fast-forwarded and deleted. They have to count. Preparing for what you are going to say before you place the call is imperative, and you have to be ready for any of the above three possibilities and be ready to switch marketing gears fast so that you don't lose an opportunity when it presents itself. If you are looking to sell your prospect on the fact that your company has creative event planning solutions that will be of value to it, that must be reflected in all you say and do, even when leaving a telephone message or speaking with your potential customer's assistant. Again, you have just 20 seconds. That does not mean that you have to get your message across in its entirety, but you do have to hook it before it make its decision to tune out.

Some sales reps, unsuccessful at reaching a potential client by telephone or having them return calls, alternately scour the client's company website looking for an e-mail address or decipher how the company e-mail addresses are assigned. It can be relatively easy to figure out a company's e-mail system in some cases. Done right, with a targeted hook, an e-mail can capture attention, as the subject line usually registers before someone hits the delete key. One mistake that is often made, despite concern about e-mail viruses, is sending an attached sales letter with nothing in the message box to identify who the e-mail is from or why it is being sent. Very few people will open an attachment from an unknown source or even send a reply to question the reason for the attachment or the e-mail being sent. A more likely possibility is that your message will be deleted and that you get placed on the blocked senders list, so that all your future e-mail gets trashed. If you are hoping to attract customers' attention by e-mail, never send an attachment unless you have been invited to, make sure that your subject line contains a hook and take care to ensure that your message states clearly why you are contacting them. Quickly introduce the potential value you bring to their company that is specific to them. A generalized value like "enhanced bottom line" is meaningless. For example, telling your prospect that the events your company has designed have produced outstanding financial results for other companies (backed up with figures and percentages but never naming names), sold out hotels or required back-to-back programs in order to accommodate all the qualifiers has more impact. Telling a client that your company has just won top industry honors for creating the best event under $50,000 or that you were the company that created the successful event that everyone in their industry is buzzing about will get their attention. Knowing what matters to their company is important. Ask what your prospect would want to receive from you. Many sales reps are focused only on what they want to give, not what the client would be receptive to. Putting clients' needs first is key. You want them to connect with what you are saying, visualize the benefits a strategic business alliance with your company will bring them and have them reaching to hit the reply button instead of the delete key.

One catering company soliciting sales and targeting event planning business for the Thanksgiving season sent out a mailing asking clients "Need to talk turkey?" as part of its 20-second attention grabber. The mailing gave the company's telephone number up front, followed with its employees' combined years of service serving up turkey, how many turkey dinners it has made, how many turkey preparations it has, and that it has a dietitian on staff to help the staff design custom menus that can meet any special dietary requirements that a planner's clients might be interested in, such as tasty, tempting low-carb or low-fat versions of more traditionally heavy fare. It met an event planning need by giving planners creative new food options with which they in turn could use to tantalize their clients. Highlighting its nutritionist on staff helped it to set itself apart from its competition. Its marketing campaign was on target, timely and very successful in attracting new and old clients.

If you are hoping to capture customers' attention by mailing your material to them, take a moment to think about how you process the mail that comes across your desk. If you are working in event planning you are part of a vibrant industry that is brimming with creativity, innovative ideas and a multitude of resources, yet much of the communication from suppliers that comes across planners' desks rates hardly more than a casual glance before being tossed aside. Some packages are never even opened before they hit the waste basket because they fail to capture a recipient's imagination or offer an inventive event planning solution. Much of the discarded information has the look and feel of being mass-produced. If it doesn't grab our attention, it is toast. Occasionally, the accompanying letters bear the competition's name and address, having been slipped into the wrong envelope! That displays a lack of attention to detail and raises a red flag to planners.

Other mailings have planners reading the brochure cover to cover and have them reaching for the telephone to hear more about what you have to offer. Those are the offerings that mirror the same techniques planners use to create their promotional material for their clients' participants, where it is essential that they capture their guests' attention. If an event planning company can't produce marketing material that will draw in potential customers when it is promoting itself, how can it be trusted to turn around and do it for the client? Do not take shortcuts when you are marketing your skills. The event planning industry can be a tough one to market to because clients are looking to be wowed and they know that custom creativity is not based on how much money you have to spend, and it is applying this understanding to corporate mailings that will help your mailing be the one that is read.

Your company website should also reflect your company's talent. Think carefully before adding cartoon characters and anything too cutesy. Is this the image you want to project to potential clients or would one depicting professional polish combined with special effects serve you better when it comes to marketing your skills? The message you put out should have consistency with your other marketing endeavors. When designing your company website keep in mind who the audience is. Will they be using high-end computers with fast Internet connections that will allow them to view Flash presentations, or does the website need to be straightforward so that everyone can access it?

A non-traditional method of placing your company in a client's path is being a quoted source in industry publications, magazines and national newspapers. Being quoted gives you credibility as an industry expert and provides you with the ability to promote yourself or your company in a positive marketing environment.

AT INDUSTRY FUNCTIONS

Trade shows, educational seminars, new product presentations, familiarization trips and award presentations are all times when potential clients, event planning companies and suppliers come together in business social situations. Make a public misstep and you can kill your company's chances with a potential client. One event planning company made a major faux pas when it decided to party as a group after a trade show. The staff hired a limousine so they could take in as many post-show events as possible and came dressed in outfits that identified their company by name. The partying was hearty and this group fell into the category of guests gone wild; their behavior was boorish and several members of the group were visibly intoxicated. What they forgot was that the after-parties were open to clients as well as event planning companies and suppliers. Eyebrows were raised at their antics and more than one potential customer was heard to make note of their company name and place them mentally on their personal no-call list.

Industry events are not the time or the place to do a hard company sell, but subtle soft selling goes on all the time. They can be used as a venue to market your professionalism and display your company's creativity. For example, if your group is up for an award for producing an outstanding event, you will be basking in the reflected spotlight and clients who attended the award show—pay attention to who is there—will be open to taking calls from the winners who now have a proven history of successfully helping their other clients look good. They may actively seek out members of your team to ask for a business card.

If your company is exhibiting at a trade show, make sure that you maximize the marketing opportunities and bring your best to the table. Come prepared. Make backup plans in case you run out of material on the first day. Make sure that you know the past history of the show and the number of attendees that have come in the past. Many trade shows provide a list of registered guests, which should be reviewed in advance. Confirm you have plenty of business cards, keep samples and a full set of promotional material for display purposes only and mark it so it is not given away, ensure that you have a back-up plan in place to capture names and address of attendees so that you can send requested material out to them when you get back to the office, and research options on how quickly you can bring in more material. To go through the cost of having a booth and not being on top of what you need can present your company in a negative light. Make sure that what you bring is targeted to the audience that will be attending the trade show and is in keeping with your company image. If you begin to cut back or reduce your visibility at trade shows you've always attended, it could be interpreted to mean that your company is in trouble. The reality may be that you are switching marketing gears, and if so, that you have some exciting new plans in the works—build anticipation.

Use the social setting to mix, mingle and market yourself and your company by introducing yourself to others. Connect with your host instead of staying within your comfort zone with your office buddies—you can socialize with them at work tomorrow. You never know when a meeting by chance will turn out to be the catalyst for moving forward with a client. A supplier raving about your company's abilities as he introduces you to someone he thinks you should meet can open a door that was closed before. And you will never learn more if you don't expand your horizons and meet new people.

Give serious consideration to taking part in any industry charity sports event. Golf tournaments, for example, are a great opportunity to get to know clients on a different level, and those who are on top of their game are sought-after partners for foursomes. Remember, tennis, sailing, basketball and racquetball are universal "business sports" and valuable skills to know, and are not limited to a specific gender. One female planner dazzled the crowd at charity pool tournaments. She had taken lessons from a pro, knew a few trick moves and had potential clients gathered around her clamoring for advice on how to improve their game. Knowledge of baseball, football and hockey is also beneficial in social chitchat with business executives. Opportunities to take part in sporting events will come up on familiarization trips, on site inspections and traveling with the group. The sport you choose to learn dictates whether or not you will be the one left behind. Being the one who can step in and play can help give you and your company a competitive edge. Do you really want to watch your client on a golf course with your competition one-on-one for five or more hours, and miss a chance to market yourself and your company and get the upper selling hand?

WHERE THEY PLAY SOCIALLY

An event planning company owner who handled the financial market and also was involved in contributing his talents as a volunteer to gala fundraisers noticed many of his client's brokers were attending an upscale charity function his company was not putting on. The brokers were using the event to contribute to a good cause and market themselves as they moved about the room. They had mastered putting themselves in a rich environment and knew how to make the most of it. The planner, on the other hand, wasn't, and was missing out on a major marketing moment. At this event he was putting his professional reputation in a precarious position. He had not thought about the role he was playing at the event; he was there in the capacity of a setup volunteer, called in at the last moment when there were a number of no-shows. He had not been part of event coordination and this event was running badly, one visible disaster after another. His client's guests saw him there and assumed that the event was one of his designs, which did not reflect well on him. Guests were quite vocal about the delays and disorganization. Perception is everything and this event was being perceived as being a train wreck. At one point the volunteers who had showed up were conscripted into clearing the dishes. The fundraising committee had forgotten to hire waitstaff and the event was a wine and food tasting. The committee members had also neglected to factor in guests using multiple plates, glasses and silverware. The problem was compounded by chefs using wine glasses to serve the dessert and the fact that the dishwasher at the venue did not have a large capacity.

The event planner learned a valuable lesson from the guests: that putting yourself in a target-rich environment where your clients are is a business-building marketing endeavor. But it has to be done right. The capacity in which you are taking part in an event must be as a guest or playing a key role, and must not compromise the integrity of what you do professionally.

There are many occasions where event planning companies and their staff can be involved in events at which potential clients may be attending, partying and playing. One event planner met one of her company's best clients running a marathon. They shared a real common interest and it opened the door to conversation and much more. Another planner met one of her clients at a fashion show where they both shared a passion for clothes. Someone else met one of his clients while whale watching by kayak. What brought them together was a love of adventure. Film festivals, the theater—especially if you upgrade to VIP tickets with access to the private lounge during intermission—sporting events, concerts, art exhibits and gallery showings are all potential business playgrounds.

CREATED OPPORTUNITIES

You can also market to your potential clients by playing host. You can create opportunities to bring a select group of people together. Whatever you do must be in keeping with the quality of work that you do, be targeted to your audience and have a return on your investment (monetary or otherwise). Airlines, hotels, tourist boards, destination management companies, venues and suppliers all pull together, sharing costs, to create a marketing opportunity when they put together a familiarization trip. They are creating an event that will showcase their companies and their products in a favorable light, put them in a target-rich environment and provide them with chance to develop their client relationships outside of the office. Their expected return on their investment is new business and word-of-mouth promotion upon their guests' return.

One event planner loves to pull together top business executives for lunch and does it not one at a time but as a very select gathering. She brings in a well-known guest speaker she knows holds the clout to draw busy company heads away from their work during the middle of their day. The luncheons are such a success that rarely do her guests return to the office. She is providing them with an event that holds great appeal and one that enhances her reputation.

She also does theater evenings for her clients, inviting them as her guests for cocktails, dinner, the theater and decadent dessert post show. For her more active clients she arranges flyfishing expeditions and is an active participant on her weekend getaways. She woos her clients to her side by appealing to all of their sides. She makes sure that they can relate on many levels and she knows what drives their event planning decisions. She also involves the spouses on the flyfishing weekends and theater evenings to make sure that they are not left behind. She creates these events specifically to market herself and her company but does it unobtrusively, and doing so has been a fruitful venture personally and professionally.

There are many ways to connect with clients in and out of the office. Some situations are appropriate for hard sells, such as when you have been invited to present, while others are soft-sell marketing opportunities where you will be able to introduce yourself to new clients and open a door that may have been closed before. Be open to new ventures that could hold business and promotional possibility. The cost is a business investment. They could be work or play related and take place in a boardroom, a ballroom, or a theater or on a golf course or the deck of boat in your home city or across the world. Everyone in the company can be trained to look for new ways to market what they do. Marketing is not limited to sales representatives or company owners, and in fact it should not be left to them alone. Some event planning companies pay their internal and external staff (freelance program directors) for business leads. A number of opportunities can actually take place during one of your events. Always remember that guests attending an event are also potential clients, and many staff members are approached on site for a contact name; make sure that you are prepared for that, that staff on site know who to direct a referral to and that follow-up is timely.

Questions to consider when looking to market effectively to your audience include:

- Does my promotional material have energy?

- Does it project the right company image to the clients I am targeting?

- Am I guilty of sending introductory form letters out to clients instead of customizing them to address their specific needs?

- How effective have my present marketing efforts been in turning targeted clients into customers?

- Do I have 20-second opening statements prepared that will catch a prospective client's attention?

- Have I clearly defined my business platform?

- Do I know what hook will draw client interest and make them want to do business with me?

- Does my marketing message have a sharp focus?

- What opportunities am I overlooking that would allow me quality time to interact with clients?

- What event planning techniques could I incorporate into my marketing campaign?

8

SOLICITING SALES

Innovative Ideas

If your hope is to create events that will excite guests, you must first be able to excite your clients-to-be. In order to open a door that will get you through their front door, you must first get their attention. Clients are weary of being inundated by sales representatives who waste their valuable time by giving them a tired song-and-dance routine. Sales representatives may cling to old methods, such as reading from their sales kit over the telephone, sending said sales kit as follow-up, and then, if they should be lucky enough to meet with the client, sitting them down and repeating the same message over again. Reps who do this are very likely to be shown the door, not have it opened further.

The event planning sales process usually begins with a "cold call" or "warm lead." A cold call is one where the sales rep has had no prior contact with the client or his company. They are starting off from square one. They are an unknown identity to the customer. Some sales reps like to initiate their client contact over the telephone, introduce themselves and their company, make a general query regarding the type of business and events they do, hope to sell the client on their services and ask if they can send their sales kit material to them for further review or set up a meeting to come by in person. Others prefer to send their material out first with an introductory letter and either state a time that they will be calling the client to follow up or ask the client to call them at their convenience.

A warm lead is one where the sales rep may have been referred to a specific person by a business or personal contact. The client may not have heard of the sales rep or her company but would be familiar with the person or company that gave the referral and may be more inclined to be receptive and take the time to hear what she has to say. Some sales reps feel more comfortable with a warm lead, while others, even though they may have been given someone's name by one of their contacts, prefer to call the prospective client without dropping names—as a cold call, wanting to succeed on their own merit.

These are exactly the same techniques that suppliers in the event planning field use when soliciting your business, and it is not very effective. You only have to ask yourself how many sales kits have you thrown out, how many sales calls have you not returned or how many meetings you and other staff members have come out of saying, "What a waste of my time."

A sales kit is a presentation piece; it is in essence your company's press kit. It must reflect the image you want to project as a company and be a match for the clients your company is selling to. While it outlines your qualifications, a sales kit does not tell clients how you can meet their specific needs.. To the client this is the same trite message they hear over and over again from everyone wanting to do business with them. It has become meaningless.

What a client can deduce from your company's presentation kit is the quality of care that goes into your work, whether or not it is polished and professional or pieced together and an overview of your company's credentials—that is the sum of what it represents to them. To a client, your company's sales kit is a marketing tool viewed as a public relations package, not a medium to close a sale. It can, if done right, get you through the door, but the same message the kit contains is not what clients want to hear once a sales representative is sitting in front of them.

If you want to gain the competitive edge, it is important to capture clients' attention with your creativity and original approach in a way that is meaningful to them, because after all, isn't that exactly what you are trying to sell them on? If you want clients to tune in to what your company has to offer you must target your sales pitch to fit their needs and explain by what means your company can be their solution. Put yourself in your customers' shoes and see what they see, hear what they hear and ask whether or not your message, as it is being delivered, is meaningful or meaningless to them. For example, don't hide behind that the old sales cliché of saying that you can do "whatever it takes to win their business." That is an empty phrase. What clients want to hear is *how* you can help them to compete in their marketplace. They are looking for someone who can devise a means by which their customers will sit up and take notice of them. Clients are looking for marketing and motivational support that will set them apart from their competition. They are seeking creative options that will give their company a competitive edge and are looking to see a display of your talents. To a client, one sales prerequisite is seeing that ability exhibited before they entrust their company's success to you. If your company cannot devise a way to stand out from your competition and give yourself a competitive edge, how can they have confidence that you can deliver? Billions of dollars are spent every year on event marketing solutions and customers want to know that they are working with a company that will bring them a return on their investment. When you are speaking with clients or sending them information, your company's credibility is on the line and in their hands. Make your message meaningful and ensure it matters to them.

You can capture clients' attention when soliciting sales by appealing to their senses, using the exact same techniques event planners use when they are creating clients' teaser campaigns, promotion materials and events. Event planners know what to do; they just need to do a turnaround and apply the same principles they use to create successful events to their marketing endeavors. That is where many companies falter—they prepare something that is standard issue and lose track of the importance of coming from a creative perspective where it is needed most, has the most value to their success and can gain them a competitive edge.

Meet clients where it matters most to them—on their business playing field—and become their creative solution. Look for ways to creatively break through the mountains of information they receive every day and capture their attention. One company even stream-rolled its message on a beach—meeting its clients where they were. Move away from the mundane and ordinary because that is not what you are selling. Personalize your marketing campaign to the appropriate industry, in a manner that clients are likely to respond to, in a way that highlights your company's abilities and which will draw them to you by:

- Creating Sales Opportunities in Unconventional Ways
- Bringing About an Emotional Response
- Captivating a Client with Creative Concepts

CREATING SALES OPPORTUNITIES IN UNCONVENTIONAL WAYS

An event planning company owner who was heavily involved in promoting sales for her company knew that the company possessed amazing talent that would be of great value to the entertainment industry. Its sales kits were laid out in a manner that was industry specific and more along the lines of a cutting-edge press kit. It really captured attention and demonstrated that the company was in tune with its industry. The staff had prepared a professional message with the help of scriptwriters and a voice coach and had undergone professional training in how to conduct a client interview. Where they were out of step was in their personal style. The look the staff presented said staid and was more suited to banking than the entertainment industry. While their talent and material was very original, image in all things was of the utmost importance. They decided to take a page from their main client and invested in a well-known stylist, hair and make-up artist in their client's industry to come and show them how to dress for success in this specialized market. They knew they were masters in the art of helping people look the part, but they needed sophistication with an edge. The stylist actually went out and selected starter outfits for each of them and went through their individual wardrobes to advise them on what would work and what wouldn't. The fashion and style nuances they were shown added to their total package and helped them open doors, go through doors and close sales in their chosen field. They now looked like what they said they could do, which enhanced their attraction factor to clients.

One company, with offices across the country, was looking to increase its sales, company loyalty and company goodwill. It asked its independent sales staff to contribute to setting up a local charity golf event at an exclusive golf course where the winners got to play on a course that held great appeal and support their favorite charities at the same time. The charity golf tournament was the staff's sales and marketing tool to bring select clients to them. It would enable them to introduce themselves to prospective clients in a non-intrusive way—they were not approaching them with a sales pitch for their company. The company could choose specific clients to invite to take part in the tournament; have control of setting up the golf foursomes so that it could have its key staff members on teams, which would give them quality time with the clients they were looking to connect with; show off the event planning style and expertise with running an event; get media attention; garner client and community goodwill; and do something good in the process. It wanted to stand out from its competition, which was just doing in-office sales presentations; give back to the communities in which its clients lived; provide its sales staff with a way to meet potential clients and do so in a way that everyone came away a winner looking forward to participating again the next year; and have a return on its investment by turning new contacts into clients. In turn, it gave its clients an opportunity to look good by being involved with a fundraising endeavor, provided them with an opportunity for positive press and opened the door for the event planning company's sales reps to call on them.

One fast-food company that prided itself on being responsive to trends saw its sales slipping away when its clients began focusing on becoming health conscious and moving away from what had to offer. It was quick to create new product options and teamed with a well-known fitness expert to endorse and promote the company—giving credibility to its product—and encouraged its customers to commit to their new lifestyle by including a pedometer with purchases from its healthy new menu selections. It showed its clients that it listened to what was important to them and cared about their welfare, and created a reason for them to return to its stores. Another fast-food company used a different sales tactic and put to use its website to market its commitment to customers' health and well-being. Their website featured a food calculator that let its customers add and subtract ingredients and toppings so that they could get the exact nutritional information for any menu item prepared the way they liked it.

A museum that wanted to attract a new audience and increase sales to its facility created an event that became a much-anticipated yearly event. The music, dancing and exhibits it brought in were targeted to entice a specific crowd. Tickets to its event became one of the most sought-after events of the summer. The museum captured both client and media attention. Merely making sales calls or using its promotional dollars to take out ads would not have produced the same results. Its objective in creating this event, which was a sales and marketing tool, was to introduce a new clientele to its facility. It chose to create an experience that would get its community buzzing, and entice younger guests to attend, see what it had to offer and hopefully lure them into returning to the museum when it had other exhibits.

One outdoor sporting event, hoping to draw record crowds, captured media attention to help its event promote ticket sales. It promised that it would do everything possible to ensure that it would not rain on its festivities and did cloud seeding (authorized by officials) so that rain would be induced away from the city on that day. The media attention's regarding the novelty aspect of the cloud seeding helped to promote sales to the sporting event and drew its customers' attention to what was taking place in a different way. Had it merely taken out an ad promoting its event, it would not have had the turnout it enjoyed, which was scheduled to take place rain or shine.

A supplier just starting out, determined to make her mark in floral designs, began with little more than business cards and one exquisite specialty arrangement she had designed and packaged as a delivery. She decided to market her business and solicit sales by putting herself in a target-rich environment—her city's financial district and upscale shopping area—and simply carried her arrangement up and down elevators and out on the street. She was stopped by passersby to find out who had created such a beautiful display, and had her business cards at the ready. When she returned back to her "office," which was her basement, she was in business, with people having already called to place orders. What she had created held such appeal and it was filling a client need for something new and fresh.

One event planning company used a fascinating brick-shaped light called the Tumbler, which changes color when it is turned. Its message to one of its clients looking to increase its market share was that its company could be the one to light the way for it with creative options. Its hook was sending something new to pique client interest and something that tied into its sales and marketing message. Something similar could be done for companies where safety is their focus, using the new battery-operated wax candles (Candle Safe, www.greatideas.ws) that are being used in luxury hotels in Las Vegas and by a major television network on its television shows.

Several designers came together to create an event that would showcase their designs, help them tie their brand to an upscale image, grab headlines that would bring them international publicity, and spark interest and sales in their clothing line. Their marketing approach was to sponsor individual debutantes from high society— and dress them in their couture gowns—for "coming out" debutante balls. A debutante ball presents girls usually between the ages of 15 and 19 to society and announces to the world that they are ready to be courted.

BRINGING ABOUT AN EMOTIONAL RESPONSE

A hotel chain used humor to sell its guest rooms to clients. It captured the media's fancy by offering a "towel amnesty" under which all would be forgiven if clients submitted stories about the towels that had gone missing from its hotels over the years. In return, the hotel was offering to donate money to charity for each story submitted. And it also had special edition towels made up as a promotional gift to clients staying at its hotels over a specified weekend date.

Another hotel's sales team was quick off the mark to capture the attention of a nation. When newspapers reported that Governor Jeb Bush said an offer of asylum might be a good idea for a fan who played a key role in the Chicago Cubs' collapse in Game 6 of the National League Championship Series by trying to grab a foul ball, an oceanfront retreat offered him a free three-month stay if he needed to get out of Chicago until all the hubbub died down. While it was unlikely that the fan would actually take them up on the extended offer, the publicity that it rendered for their hotel through humor and empathy stood out as newspapers and newscasts throughout North America picked up the story.

A fitness club did exactly the same thing. A top television show, with millions of viewers, issued a weight loss challenge to its audience at large and future shows, and announced it would focus on selected guests who had accepted the weight loss challenge and follow their progress throughout the year. The fitness club aligned itself with the show and free memberships with personal trainers were provided for the weight loss challenge members. It received excellent marketing and PR exposure on the show, the company name was mentioned on air seemingly once a week and many of the weight loss challenge members were filmed at its clubs working out. It tied its brand and its professional credibility to the television host, which was an excellent promotional move. Then it upped the ante. When the show received queries from hundreds and hundreds of audience members across the country expressing their difficulty finding places for the support groups they had formed to meet, the fitness company, which had multiple gyms across North America, offered its facilities free of charge at any time to the weight loss support groups. For a gym looking to sign up new members, what better way was there to introduce your facilities to a target group that had expressed a desire to get fit and had a need that the fitness company could fill? It was a marketing venture that would bring potential clients right to the front door. It then took its marketing efforts to an even higher level by offering a two-week complimentary VIP club membership at local gyms to everyone in the audience and viewers at home. A top-of-the-line fitness equipment manufacturer also got involved and received marketing benefits by giving away its product to the weight loss challenge members. Its company name was repeatedly mentioned, its product displayed on the show and it had the backing and endorsement of the show's host. Both companies were reaching millions of viewers, marketing themselves to potential customers and positioning themselves in a good light by showing their support and encouragement to people who had expressed a burning desire to lose weight. This was an emotion many viewers at home could relate to.

One company used a specially prepared marketing kit to bring a smile, display a creative spark and attract new customers. Its folder was covered in negative headlines and it promoted the company as the antidote to bad news. The company wanted to attract its clients' attention creatively, and send a message that it could help its customers produce good results and good news for their company.

Think of the possibilities when marketing your services to clients. For example, for clients in the architectural field, a possible event take-home gift or a part of a teaser mailing could be specialty pieces from famed architect Frank Lloyd Wright's masterpiece home, Fallingwater. As part of a fundraising effort for renovations, the Western Pennsylvania Conservancy that owns the home created jewelry from the bits and pieces of concrete that were removed. The concrete is embedded with silver in a clear resin and showcases the imaginativeness of the architectural field as well.

For clients considering San Francisco as a destination or clients for which an "escape from" theme might tie in should note that the National Park Service is selling off chunks of Alcatraz. It is renovating decaying cells and guard quarters. Rather than ferrying tons of rubble, it found a way to make money. The promotional piece tied to a theme may serve to attract interest.

One company used moxie marketing in its approach. It included in its promotional marketing piece a videotape, a nutcracker and two walnuts. The nutcracker and the two walnuts were a tongue-in-cheek reference to the message it put across in the video about a character being a hard nut to crack, and it made recipients smile and remember the company, which was its intent.

Sales zoomed through the roof for clients in the pet shop industry when they teamed with movie theaters to set up displays in their foyers when Disney's *Nemo* film was released. That was emotional marketing. Parents and children alike were enchanted by the displays. The pet shops were set up with displays as well, and they were prepared well in advance to avoid missing an amazing sales opportunity.

One company used a fresh approach to introduce its new staff member. It served as an introduction, and as a display of its sense of fun and its creativity. The employee had gone to a local shopping mall and had her picture taken in an old-fashioned photo booth where your photograph comes out in a strip. She made a variety of poses with different expressions and took the handful of photo strips back to her company. It combined all the images in a post-card format and invited its clients to "meet the many faces" of its newest employee. The response was better than expected. The cost was minimal. The company's creativity and sense of fun shone through and spoke volumes.

A small island in the Pacific, looking to increase sales and capture its clients' imagination, opened the first underwater post office, which is manned by postal workers in diving gear. It has waterproof postcards for sale and an underwater postage franking machine. To event planning clients who have an interest in underwater fantasy adventure, this destination would lend itself to a special mailing that would stand out. It would also be a fun mailing piece to clients who you know have a personal interest in scuba diving and would be sure to elicit a return telephone call.

One company received national attention by surprising its employees with holiday bonuses that were totally unexpected. It wanted to thank its staff in a meaningful way, giving employees a bonus of $1,000 for each year they worked at the company. Some received company bonuses of up to $20,000 and even the newest employees were taken care of. The media found out about the goodwill gesture and the company received incredible exposure. How the company was portrayed, and the kind remarks from its staff and the community, had people everywhere wishing to feel as valued as those employees were. In turn, the gesture the company made ended up having incredible marketing value thanks to people—including potential customers and suppliers—feeling goodwill towards the company.

Another company touched people's hearts through a goodwill promotion that brought them incredible marketing value, positioning itself as a company that is caring, has compassion, can create memories that will last a lifetime and has interesting connections. The company provided charter planes to take terminally ill children and their families on a one-hour flight to the North Pole. They were going to connect with Santa, who would be traveling by sleigh to meet them. The cockpit doors opened midway through the flight to reveal that Santa had arrived, and he walked up and down the aisles to greet each child. The joy and wonder on the children's faces were captured on film and picked up by the media. Their happiness and excitement leapt off the television screen right into viewers' hearts. This was replayed across the country, as the company ran repeated the flights to the North Pole in order to accommodate as many children as possible.

Emotion—heartstring, humor and desire—can be a powerful marketing tool when it is targeted to a client's need. For example, for several years the cell phone market was in a slump, then technology turned its world upside down and sales were skyrocketing again. Introducing the next generation of cell phones, those with color screens, camera phones and smart phones, gave people who had been satisfied with their old cell phone a reason to buy a new one. Savvy cell phone companies immediately launched undercover marketing campaigns and placed models posing as tourists or happy couples in trendy locations to stop people and ask them to take their picture with their cell phone, thereby positioning themselves to demonstrate the cell phone's picture-taking abilities. The cell phone companies hoped that by using undercover marketing techniques to place their product literally in the hands of their targeted market and by showing them how easy their product was to operate, they would achieve one or more marketing goals, which included attracting consumer interest, creating a desire to own the product and creating a viral/virus marketing effect (which is spreading word of the product by one person telling two people, who each tell two people, and so on, creating product buzz). The camera cell phones became extremely popular. An event planning company that specialized in high-end incentives for companies whose industry demanded that they have all the latest toys was able to use the camera cell phone as an entry for a meeting with a client who was looking for an incentive program. It incorporated the new phones into the client's promotional launch and sent the sales force visual images, taken during the site inspection. It included the message that they could put themselves in the picture. The cell phones, combined with the program, captured the client's attention and was successful in creating desire from the sales force to be on that beach, cell phone in hand, sending back photos to the office.

One supplier had no need to advertise her products. Her bags did it for her. She had perfected putting images on quality leather goods, and turning favorite photos into one-of-a-kind diaper bags, cosmetic bags and handbags. The bags could be incorporated into a teaser mailing or take-home gift for clients. Her product had the "aah" emotional factor and everyone who saw them wanted to know where to purchase them.

Enhanced CDs were the marketing mode for one company. It used mini CDs (that could be played and contained a musical message that promoted the company) in the lids of soft drink cups (the straw fit through the center) to get its message across in a memorable way at its event created to target the music industry. It used a product the client could relate to, in a way that was different, and helped it market its creativity.

CAPTIVATING A CLIENT WITH CREATIVE CONCEPTS

One event planner won accounts by being ahead of her competition and giving herself a competitive edge. The moment she heard of an event that would be perfect for her talents, she was on top of it. While other companies were in the discussion stages of what to send, within 24 hours she had put together her creative concept and had it on the client's desk. Simply sending over a fax of her ideas—with her client's permission—landed a major account. The client was captivated by her creative design. In the end, she devised something even better, but she won the contract because the client knew from her outline that she knew exactly what his company was trying to achieve and who the event would be targeted to. What she did was awaken her client's interest by proposing her creative concept of his company's event. She did it in a manner that stood out and where the only expenditure was her time and her ideas. She had used this marketing style effectively to solicit sales and land accounts.

Creative concepts can be built around a teaser presentation that will get your client's attention, and should be creatively packaged, tied into your event design. It should not include your sales kit. That can come later, when you meet with the client or you are invited to send it in. Always make sure that your contact information is included in an artistic way.

Note that there is no "tone" of language that's right for every client or concept. Tailor your language to appeal to each individual situation. The intent in each case is to plant a seed for a meeting and to showcase your strengths. Give the client a creative perspective of what form his or her event could take. A creative concept doesn't talk about the venue, the availability, the number of guests, costs or event logistics. Instead it focuses on the senses—what guests will see when they first walk in, what they will eat and drink as they mix and mingle, what they will hear in the background and what they will experience during dinner and after. It should be laid out in such a manner that it can be scaled up or down and should focus only on the feeling your client will want the event to bring to his guests and how you can meet his objectives through the event elements. You want the client to live the event on paper. Make sure, by having done your research, that your concept is in keeping with the client's past history or holds the potential for desire. One company that had never held events out of country could "see" the appeal of an exotic destination for its guests, and the event planning company that had piqued its interest won its next incentive with little more than an idea for a five-night incentive sent in a Asian take-out container with "learner chopsticks" (knife and fork at the end of each chopstick) and customized fortune cookies.

Creative concept examples for a corporate event, a fundraising gala and a theme event can be found in Appendix E of this book.

| T |
| I | Give thought to how mailings will be sent. One customer mailing was too big for mail slots and weight exceeded carrier weight restrictions.
| P |

The creative concept marketing approach can also be adapted to fit the needs of clients whose first concern is fiscal transparency. A sample event cost summary can be prepared to show the client visually how their event costs will be laid out. The sample cost summary sheet does not have to contain actual dollars amounts. What will be of interest to the client is seeing visually how the event expenses will be laid out and broken down. For maximum effect, the cost summary sheet is best based on a creative concept outline that is tailored to the client's event requirements. This way the client can clearly see the planner's proposed ideas, attention to detail in capturing costs and business style. Sample cost summary sheets can be found in *Event Planning: The Ultimate Guide to Successful Meetings, Corporate Events, Fundraising Galas, Conferences, Conventions, Incentives and Other Special Events* (John Wiley & Sons, 2000).

Soliciting sales using innovative ideas is an approach designed to get your client's attention, help you to stand out from your competition and give you a competitive edge. In a world of information overload, where everyone is vying for a client's business, it is important that your presentation sales approach have the power to sway client interest to your firm. Planners use strategic planning techniques every day, helping their clients to meet their event objectives. These same event planning principles can be used to plan for their sales success and meet their own company's objectives.

Daily, planners help their clients create sales opportunities in unconventional ways, bring about an emotional response from participants and captivate guest interest with event creativity. They do this by being innovative, bringing fresh ideas to their planning and their presentations to their client's targeted audience by designing teaser campaigns, motivational messages and events that will attract interest and inspire desire. Event planning companies can profit by using the exact same successful approaches planners use every day to benefit their clients to market themselves and showcase their talents.

Questions to consider when looking at innovative ways to increase your sales include:

- What event planning principles do I use to help my clients achieve their goals?

- Which ones have proven to be most successful with my clients' targeted audience?

- How could I use these same innovative techniques to benefit my company?

- Which ones would serve to attract my prospective client's interest?

- Do I know how my competition markets itself to potential customers?

- How can I use my creativity to produce unique sales opportunities?

- What could I do to inspire a client's desire to choose my company over my competition?

- What creative concept strategies can I employ that would serve to market my talents to potential new business?

- What form of marketing would work best to captivate my prospective clients?

9
THE VALUE OF DIVERSIFICATION

In recent years the event planning industry has been hit hard by world events. Event planning companies that simply sit back and wait to react to arising situations are going to be left behind in today's changing industry. Perceptive companies know they must plan ahead and be prepared in advance to deal with unexpected difficulties. They have witnessed the importance of knowing that an event planning crisis can happen at any moment and know that we no longer can predict industry challenges that lie around the corner. Threats from infectious diseases such as SARS, mad cow disease, West Nile virus and monkeypox came out of nowhere, and appeared one immediately after the other, hitting fast with major impact on those employed in the event planning and hospitality field. We also know, as in the case of mad cow disease, that such diseases can return without warning, bringing revenue sources to a screeching halt. As an industry, event planners can no longer afford to be caught unaware and unprepared. Nor can they become complacent because a perceived threat to their business and personal well-being and livelihood is not on their doorstep. There can be far-reaching consequences. For example, SARS was not only a concern for people in Hong Kong and Toronto, but for those traveling to all parts of the world as well. Visitors were warily arriving all across the country with masks and supplies of antibacterial wipes.

A very real ripple effect must be factored in today. Another unexpected twist that hurt the event planning business, one that was of great concern to planners in infected areas, was how it affected their ability to do business inside and outside their country during this time period. One overseas client insisted that all staff coming from an infected region to a noninfected area to orchestrate their on-site event production be quarantined for 10 days prior to arrival. Would your company be prepared from both a staffing and financial aspect to handle such a request at a moment's notice, or would you need to forfeit the business revenue? Both options could have dire financial repercussions to a business and an individual.

Event planning crisis management and risk assessment must now be anticipated, planned and prepared for, and part of the event planning process. There are still real threats out there, such as bioterrorism, the possibility of successive wars, country unrest, ongoing terrorist activity, the return of known or new infectious diseases and anticipated rolling power blackouts to be ready for. When SARS struck without warning, one top hotel was forced to lay off all staff who had not worked there seven-and-a-half years or longer for 90 days, and staff who had been there longer were guaranteed only one day's work a week during that time period. At another hotel, employees who had been there over 20 years were being laid off. Hotel occupancy fell to less than 20 percent. One hotel took a stand. Its employees were in need and it looked for ways to help them. The hotel offered free rooms over a weekend, in exchange for a $50 donation to the laid-off workers, in order to help its staff get by until they received their first employment insurance checks, which had a six-week wait period. That act had an unintended positive marketing effect thanks to the media coverage it received. The hotel's show of concern and character for its employees spilled over into community goodwill, and support as the economy rebounded. Consumers concluded that if a hotel demonstrates that much care for its employees, it stands to reason it will take good care of its hotel guests as well and be a company that customers and suppliers will want to align themselves with.

Every event planning company now knows that along with planning events and its marketing campaigns it must devise new ways to create financial independence for continued success and the company's, employees' and customers' well-being. Event planning companies are now facing the responsibility of creating a strong economic environment in order to ensure that they can financially weather anything world events or business conditions put forward.

Many event planning companies and their suppliers are masters of projecting event costs and managing their clients' budgets. Their primary focus has been on providing creative event options to meet their customers' objectives, coordinating events, serving clients and soliciting new sales. Target marketing for many was a new venture. Several companies found themselves at one time or another juggling client receivables with their payroll and other expenses, and running pretty close to the edge financially. When companies of longstanding began closing their doors or found themselves on the brink of going under because of loss of business due to world events, it was evident that attention had to be paid not only to being financially savvy with their clients' money but their own as well.

Some companies had their accountants actively seeking creative ways to manage their cash flow and maximize interest potential, for example, having a client pay by check, investing the money in short-term deposits and paying the supplier by credit card to gain 30 days before paying in full. Unfortunately, that was not enough to save companies from financial disaster when industry conditions spun out of control. What was being required of them next was to create diverse streams of income for personal and professional financial independence and financial freedom.

Diverse streams of income can be created by being on top of your cash flow and maximizing revenue returns on existing funds, controlling spending and increasing income sources. Of the three, increasing income sources can be the most financially rewarding, as there is no cap on earning potential except for the one you place on yourself.

In the event planning industry, proven strategies that produce diverse streams of income include:

• Widening Your Existing Client Base

• Expanding Your Market

• Generating New Income Sources

WIDENING YOUR EXISTING CLIENT BASE

A mistake many event planning companies make is limiting their target market to one main industry. It is a very dangerous practice to place all your eggs in one basket. If something major occurs in that one industry and its event planning requirements come to a standstill, companies handling that field find themselves in trouble. As well, events on the books may be at risk if the company does not have the funds to meet day-to-day expenses and payroll and keep its business afloat until the event takes place. For example, if one company chooses to cancel its event, anticipated future revenue from its event is no longer there. The income received by the event planning company to date may have already been spent and the cancellation penalty may not necessarily bring in more money, and depending on how far ahead the event has been cancelled, what the event planning has received to date may be all that it will be receiving. If an event planning company was in the financial position of needing the rest of the revenue from the cancelled event—which comes in staggered increments—to carry it forward until other money comes in from other companies, future payment schedules will be in dire straits. The revenue generated by existing business may not be sufficient to handle all of those needs, as events can be booked well into the future, although the most recent trend has been events with a fairly quick turnaround.

For the financial health of your company, it is important to widen your existing client industry base. This will create a diverse stream of income. Your company will be in a much stronger position from having diversified its client list. That does not mean you should stop your company's marketing efforts to your target audience. It means widen the circle and look to see what other industries would be a perfect fit for your talents. It takes time to research, develop, market and cultivate a new industry and more time to make your presence known.

Do it when conditions are good; companies cannot afford to wait for a downturn to start looking for new business.

One very successful event planning company owner started her business with this thought top of mind. She made sure that her sales representatives understood the value of diversity, as it would affect their incomes as well. She sat with them, reviewed their client lists and pointed out areas where there were weaknesses. By working closely with her salespeople to protect their financial interests, she was also protecting hers. They continued to excel in their main target areas, which was the financial industry, but slowly built up their client lists to include clients in diverse markets such as the automotive, pharmaceutical, medical and real estate industries. The revenue from these other sources ended up surpassing that of what they had considered their main revenue source. These other industries were a good fit for their company and their abilities. They had identified their strengths as handling corporate client requirements and looked specifically for industries that did more than one type of event. The clients they targeted all did meetings, conferences, trade shows, incentives, client appreciation events, award presentations and annual shareholder meetings, and some of them did special events such as new product launches and press events as well.

They wanted to play the odds when it came to diversifying. They reasoned that if a company or an industry as a whole was experiencing hardships that it may cancel its incentive programs, but it might need to keep a company conference. When the financial industry was experiencing difficult times they were still in a position of financial strength, unlike their competitors who had not had the foresight to diversify. The event planning company that had diversified also received an added bonus. It was able to snap up talented staff that had been laid off from companies going through financial difficulties.

The company owner also paid attention to different industries' cyclical patterns so that they did not encounter slow periods or times when they had to turn away business because they had more than they could handle for a specific time period. She also wanted to ensure that income was being generated year-round. For example, financial companies often did incentive programs and meetings in May and November, while car manufacturers did their product launches in September and incentive programs in February.

When widening your existing client base, one key factor to take into consideration is how difficult it will be to implement. The event planning company that had diversified knew that for maximum benefit and marketability, time and training had to be invested to bring its sales reps and the internal staff up to speed on the new industries they were taking on. The owner wanted to be more than a fulfillment house to their clients and wanted to become a vital creative and motivational resource for their customers. Her sales staff wanted to be privy to client marketing meetings, where they could offer their customers insightful industry information that might help them when considering their options. They had no resistance to taking on in-depth learning about the new industry and they did it as a team. When an opportunity presented itself, they were able to speak knowledgeably, and address client budget concerns and returns on investment strategies as related to their client's specific industry. When one new client asked for his sales rep's input on the value of her company's travel incentive programs and to compare travel incentive to merchandise rewards, he was fully prepared. Having researched his client's industry and being familiar with what his client's competition was doing, the information he had to share on the pros and cons of doing each type of program was very relevant. In this case, travel was still a powerful motivator and the upscale style of incentive trips that were taking place in the client's industry were attracting employees to the industry, helping companies retain them and bringing great returns on investment.

The event planning company also had to prepare to take on marketing on several levels. Its planners could no longer focus their energies on just one industry and had to develop an understanding of marketing to a variety of client industries. Among other things, to be more successful in their marketing approach this meant preparing promotional material that would display their talents and their company to clients in the language they spoke. Every industry has its own language that is specific to its field. It is important to develop an understanding of the terms that are pertinent to an industry so that you can converse with companies in their language. Clients and their staff members do not have the time nor the interest in learning event planning lingo. They want their suppliers to speak to them clearly in terms they understand.

EXPANDING YOUR MARKET

If expanding your market is a consideration, you need to make sure that the area you choose to develop is compatible with your existing business so that you don't end up jeopardizing one for the other.

One event planning company found the perfect match for personal and professional desires and company growth and achieved great success when it set out to expand its market reach. The owner started out working for another event planning company to gain experience before opening his own event planning company, which catered to high society. His focus was on social-based events and not business, and he had no desire to expand into that market. His staff had a natural ability with theme decor and often opted to create their own room displays without using the services of decor or prop rental companies. By using their own designs they were able to put a distinctive stamp on the events they created. They purchased their own props and soon amassed a good inventory in their warehouse. This enabled them to set up a different division of their company and rent their props to other event planning companies. So that there would be no confrontations about conflict of interest, they were upfront with the event planning companies and did not hide their involvement. Generally, they marketed their product to event planning companies whose client base was corporate and in areas in which they did not work. Event planning companies interested in renting the company's props and table settings were reassured that the owners were expanding their business by moving in a new direction and were not trying to take over their corporate clients or acquire insider knowledge. They were working in true partnership.

To increase their event planning business and market their decor company expansion to their society audience, the event planners became deeply involved with gala fundraising events. They knew this was a target-rich environment in which to network and display their talents. While they volunteered their expertise to the fundraising chair and committee heads, they did not donate their props and table decor because there were real hard costs for transportation and labor for the shipping, set-up and tear down of their displays and they needed to be fiscally responsible to their business. As a compromise and area of negotiation, they made their decor stock available at cost in exchange for an ad in the event program and a complimentary table of 10 so that they could then market their designs to their invited guests, who they hoped were future customers. They expanded their market by marketing their event planning services to society patrons and their decor company to both their society patrons and the event planning market. They had a competitive edge on event planning companies who handled the society market because they owned their own props, and they were able to offer to clients at a special cost any decor they had on hand that was then adapted for use at future events.

But they did not stop there. Their subsequent company expansion involved merging their business with a company that opened the door to doing international social events. They expanded not only their market but also their reach. By finding a match for their abilities, in a company that had established itself in the desired market, they now had the capabilities and the credibility to take on the world. Several of their clients had homes around the world and wanted their event planning company of choice to design their events wherever they went. The other company had the infrastructure to handle the event logistics and guest travel arrangements, while their company was still responsible for the event design and would oversee production and be on site to orchestrate the actual event.

Next on their expansion list was acquiring a forgotten venue that they knew they could transform into a sought-after one, one that could be used for their own society events, marketed to the event planning companies that were using the services of their decor company, be a venue consideration for gala fundraising events and be the perfect vehicle for holding press conferences. They did not go into this venture looking to create a market; they came to the venture with their market fully developed.

After that, their plan involved moving into the lighting and audio-visual field. They did their research and acquired a company that could handle the special needs of their clients and had an extremely talented staff. The abilities of the communication company's staff were a match for their designs. Together they were capable of creating outstanding special effects.

The event planning company knew its industry, its product and its possibilities. It had developed its market and expanded it in a way that each venture complemented the next. It built a strong foundation on which to move its expansions forward, and in each case it carefully reviewed its risk factor. It covered its bases in making itself marketable to clients and to what others might have billed its competition. It diversified and instead of fighting to survive, it thrived. And its staff did it all while doing what they loved to do best. It branched out with new products, expanded its market and did it successfully.

GENERATING NEW INCOME SOURCES

Some companies choose to diversify by generating new income sources. Alcoholic beverage manufacturers, for example, trying to attract a younger market, started infusing their product with fruit flavors. This became a global trend and soon manufacturers of rum, vodka, tequila and other popular alcoholic drink choices were all offering an array of products. They still had their main audience, which preferred its beverage of choice pure, but they also had a viable alternative for those looking for something new. They infused their product and their market.

Another manufacturer created a product out of what had been waste. A creative coffee manufacturer turned used coffee grounds into "Java Logs" and created a new income source that is now part of a growing multi-million-dollar industry. It is environmentally friendly, as the coffee grounds that are now an income source had previously been slated for landfills. It is also the perfect fun gift for coffee lovers, even for the name appeal alone. The product, when burned, does not give off a coffee smell but also does not give off the chemical scent that some logs do—and it is extremely marketable. The company recycled, reused and came up with a diversification winner.

One fitness company generated a new source of income by creating classes that the public would be drawn to, and that would be an innovative new activity for a corporate event. It timed the launch of its product to tie in with the premiere of a movie that featured what it had to offer. Staff knew they would have the media clamoring to talk with them and the end result would be great press. Their timing let them ride the building momentum. While their company specialized in martial arts, which are commonplace, they upped the ante on their competition by offering fitness classes in samurai training. The fitness benefits had been in the news because of the dramatic body changes they had produced in the stars of the samurai movie. They capitalized by piggyback marketing when interest in their product would be at an all-time high with the media, the public and their existing clientele. The product also held appeal to anyone who had studied fencing or marital arts. It introduced them to a new medium. What the fitness company was offering was training classes that taught students how to become one with their fitness sword and get a fantastic workout in the process. Television segments and newspaper write-ups had event planners' creative minds ticking as they saw the beauty of the movement in the samurai training. This could be developed as a fitness break during a meeting, as it would appeal to both men and women, or become a full-fledged theme evening event. By creating a new class, this company created several new income sources.

When hotels opened their doors to dogs, they were looking at generating new income sources. They were hoping to attract clients and families who would have previously vacationed at pet-friendly options. They were anxious to generate new income sources because they could no longer count on the corporate market to carry them. They had to look for new ways to attract the leisure client. Hotels make their money on guest rooms, food and beverage sales, and function space rental. These are their products. If they cannot fill their hotels, they have lost an opportunity for revenue and they will never get it back. An empty guest room or ballroom is a liability to be avoided at any cost, because the cost can be too high, as in the case of the hotel that had to lay off staff that had worked with it for over 20 years. That is a situation no one in the industry wants to see repeated. Generating new income sources is essential for survival and hotels cannot get complacent if their corporate business returns, as they now know that it can disappear in a minute.

Hotels are listening carefully to their clients and looking for ways to retain them and entice them to return more frequently. They are monitoring customer needs and responding quickly. Some hotels are generating new income sources by courting non-smokers because there was a demand they were not meeting. In the process they found out that there are some profitable side benefits. They were able to attract more customers, but other benefits included lower maintenance costs. They found that housekeeping saved time on cleaning the non-smoking rooms. In an industry where minutes matter, saving time equals saving money. Little things do make a difference. Many have heard the story of how much money an airline saved by serving one less olive in each of its salads, and saving minutes on cleaning rooms adds up too. These hotels also found that their soft goods (bedding, drapes and carpet) did not have to be replaced as often or repaired as frequently. There were fewer unsightly burns in non-smoking rooms. All of this meant an added profit bonus. They also were able to use going smoke-free as a marketing tool!

Decor companies that may have marketed themselves strictly to the business market are crossing over, opening their doors to social event planning and starting to design decor for society events, gala fundraisers, weddings and proms. They knew they had to create a better balance and diversify so that if one market slowed down, the other could pick up the slack.

Some companies formed working partnerships with others that complemented what they did and brought their combined talents and strengths to markets to do events that they could not have considered on their own. For example, one company that had amazing business contacts but handled only small events was reluctant to turn down a chance to do a very high-profile opening for a new venue. A client of one of its planners, who was also a personal friend, simply handed the event over to the company. It would involve more than 2,000 VIP guests, which was well beyond anything the company had ever done before. It was a complex affair involving major tenting, indoor and outdoor fireworks, laser shows, specialty lighting, special effects, food and beverage from opening to closing, entertainment, transportation and intricate guest logistics. Working in collaboration with an event planning company that had the talents to awe this crowd and handle the project with ease but did not have the personal contacts brought diversification to both of their businesses when they came together. It was the first of many such joint ventures. As their working relationship developed they were able to refer business to one another and worked out a referral fee that was satisfactory to both companies. The first company, seeking to find ways to open up other avenues it may have had to turn away in the past, set up the same working relationship with a renowned caterer who was skilled with upscale mid-size groups that were too small for the second event planning company to take on. The caterer was so pleased with the business that came his way that he began to refer to his benefactor, as he saw the company, as his fairy godmother. What was created as a result of looking for a way to diversify was magical and profitable for all involved.

Sometimes diversification can be brought about by simply changing how and where you do business. An innovative approach or a shifting of strategies can bring a turnabout in results when a financial crunch hits. The theater industry was one of the areas that suffered when SARS stuck Toronto in 2003. People were not willing to put themselves at risk health-wise by sitting close to others, and theaters were sitting empty even after the health risk warning had been officially lifted. Theaters, hotels, sporting events, concerts, restaurants and other key areas pulled together to offer unbelievable pricing to draw guests into the city. They were trying to attract both visitors and local residents to the city, especially families who may have found going to live theater too expensive an outing. Marketing was intense and the low prices struck a nerve, and telephones rang off the hook with bookings. The response to creative price packaging was so overwhelming that they decided to run the promotion a second time, and received the same results. It showed that there clearly was a market that was not being tapped and there was immediate response when the right promotion was offered. High theater prices, not just the fear of SARS, was what was keeping families out of the theaters, restaurants and hotel guest rooms. The positive response is a marketing blueprint to stimulate sales in slow periods and introduce the theater to new audiences. One theater production had also diversified by contracting out-of-town performances and took its cast on the road.

Companies need to feel comfortable about the direction they are proposing to take their business. They want to give their clients a powerful reason to choose to work with them. They need to feel certain they have the abilities in-house to handle new ventures or that they have access to expert consultants and qualified freelancers that match the client's standards. It is impossible to sell what you do not believe in. It is essential that you have the right people with a proven history of success who can guide your company with ease through any learning curves. Many clients would be surprised to learn how many people they work with are actually freelancers and not event planning companies' full-time employees as they assume. The freelance event planning industry is very professional, keeps company business confidential and does not advertise the fact that they are only being brought in to work on specific projects unless the event planning company introduces them in this capacity. Freelancers are very protective of their industry reputation and are equally careful about which companies they affiliate themselves with.

A successful event planning company had a major setback when it attempted to diversify by adding a communication division to its business to handle its clients' presentation requirements. The owner was unfamiliar with the industry and the potential pitfalls, and the people he hired were not leaders in their field. This new arm of the company pulled the president away from his core event planning business, which began to suffer from his inattention. Many of his clients had a personal connection with him and he no longer had the time for them. The capital required to keep the new division afloat drained the event planning side, and there were no dollars left over to invest in fulfilling their needs. Customers began drifting away and both sides of the company were placed in financial distress. Diversification that was not well thought out proved to be the company's undoing and they had to shut down the communication side of the business, plus lay off a number of long-term event planning staff.

When your industry has been shaken up, as the event planning industry was, you can do two things: use the experience a catalyst for change and growth, or hide your head in the sand and do nothing in the hopes it never happens again. But there is really only one "choice." Companies who are choosing to never again be caught financially unprepared are regrouping and thinking about where they are placing their energies and what their priorities are. They are examining the opportunities that are available to them and deciding where and how they could benefit from diversification.

Questions to ask yourself before you move forward include:

• In what areas am I marketable?

• How can diversification help my business?

• What do I need to know to determine what kind of diversification would work best for my specific business?

• How can I widen my or my company's client base?

- How can I expand my or my company's market?
- How can I generate new income sources?
- What immediate add-on services could my company incorporate into what we are already doing?
- What kind of diversification would be the best fit for my company's talents?
- What do I know about the areas that have diversification appeal?
- What expertise do my company or I bring to this area?
- What expertise will my company or I need to acquire?
- How can I market what I have to offer to customers in a way that is fresh?
- What will be compromised if I move in this direction?
- What are the financial risks involved?
- What challenges could I face?
- What investment would be required?
- How much am I prepared to invest in diversification at this time?
- How can I put myself in a target-rich environment?
- What would draw attention to my or my company's new business endeavors?
- What would I need to know in order to market effectively to new clients?
- How long could it take to see results?
- What would I need to be mindful of?
- Is this compatible with what I or my company already have in place?
- Will this action create positive energy for my business?
- How can I generate referrals?
- Do I know the currency that works in this new area? Do I know what clients really value, and can I deliver?

10

GOING OUT ON YOUR OWN–COSTS AND BENEFITS

The event planning industry is one that is brimming with creative individuals who are accustomed to pushing event planning limits in order to be the first to offer something fresh and innovative to their clients. The energy in this industry from all the combined creative minds is electric. It is an industry that can be very enticing and exciting.

Just as those in the theater find their reward by audience applause, so do those involved in event planning. Planners bask in the glow of a successful event, delighting in having achieved the client's objectives and having created a moment that will stand out forever for their client's guests. Their work, no less a production than staging a play, is done backstage as opposed to taking center stage, but both planner and actor live for the applause.

Many in the event planning field are fearless about testing their talents in new directions, open to diversification and ready to take on the next challenge. And they often have an entrepreneurial soul, which can lead them to their next big event—opening their own event planning company. There are an unprecedented number of independent event planning companies in the marketplace today, both companies started by experienced planners and a surprising number starting by recent event planning graduates. These are students who have used their time in college and university to prepare for the workforce and have pursued internships that will serve them in their own businesses and ratchet up their marketability factors. Event planning entrepreneurs are fueled by visions of:

- Personal and Professional Independence
- Financial Freedom
- Unlimited Authority

PERSONAL AND PROFESSIONAL INDEPENDENCE

The thought of having control over their destiny is what holds appeal to many entrepreneurs. It is very easy to be caught up in the event planning whirlwind, and days, months and years can pass in the blink of an eye. An event that initially seemed so far in the future can suddenly creep up on you and it is hard to pin down where the time went. By the time the event planning dust clears many planners are shocked to find out that years have passed and they haven't taken the time to invest in themselves. They are doing exactly the same job they started out with. Those working in the event planning industry always have one foot in the future and one foot in today. The demands of today come in the form of deadlines and tomorrow's dramas are looming. Planners can find themselves pulled in many directions— their working conditions, clients, suppliers and real life—and they lose personal control of their destiny. The thought of opening and operating their own event planning company can be compelling because it holds the attraction of having control over their personal and professional future. People drawn to the event planning industry are comfortable wielding control over the events they plan. They have a vision, map out a plan and then execute it to their exacting standards. When planners find themselves working for a company where their job is eating up their life, they are allowed no time to grow personally and professionally and it is beyond their control to change their working conditions, they look for options that will allow them to regain control of their life and their professional direction. They weigh the choices open to them. One alternative is to work for another company, and another is to work towards attaining personal and professional independence by opening their own event planning company. A sales representative contemplating making a move has to look carefully down the road.

FINANCIAL FREEDOM

If you are working in the event planning industry in the capacity of a sales representative, your salary is not capped. You can aspire to break industry sales records but your sales could be limited if the right players are not in place at the company you work for. Having a planning department that cannot meet your proposal needs can limit the number of clients you can present to, and that can be a point of contention for an enthusiastic sales rep, especially if planners are being kept busy producing proposals for other sales representatives who do not qualify their requirements and have a low rate of success. Visions of attaining personal financial independence and freedom become rapidly diminished if sales reps choose to stay in this situation. On the other hand, they have a proven history of being able to close sales and service clients, which they could bring to their own event planning company if they were to consider that possibility.

If they leave the company they are presently with to move to another, there may be the possibility of bringing their existing clients with them depending on the sales contract they signed, but if the same situation occurs at another company, could they move them a third time without putting their working relationship at risk? If they instead opened their own event planning company and operated as an independent event planning company, they would be moving their clients only once, and with the right people in place to prepare their proposals and operate their programs they could enhance their possibilities of achieving financial independence and freedom without the limitations put on them when working for others.

Some sales representatives choose to open their own company because of contract payment disputes and a hesitation to place themselves in potentially the same situation with another company. They want to be in control of seeing actual program expenses and know exactly where they stand financially. Not all companies are honorable in how they calculate their payments to their sales representatives and some have even been taken to court—with the salesperson being awarded a substantial settlement.

What will give those in sales pause is the timing of moving forward with opening their own company. That will be contingent with what events are on the books, the dates the events will take place, what outstanding monies they could conceivably be walking away from and how their contract is worded. For example, are there any non-compete clauses or time restraints with regard to soliciting business from existing clients? What upcoming business is close to requiring a proposal? If potential losses are significant they will not want to instigate proceedings with the company they are presently with.

UNLIMITED AUTHORITY

One event planning company got its start because of the company owner's desire to have complete control over the type of events they did, how they did them and the direction they wanted to grow in. They had done one road rally too many for the company they worked for, events were being recycled and the company was out of control. Caught up in day-to-day demands, they found themselves in a case of not seeing the forest for the trees until they carved out a moment to take a breath and really look at the situation at hand. What prompted this was an offer to the employee from the company owner to buy into her company. The employees' immediate response was "no, your standards are not mine" and this was spoken aloud. They knew that they were at a crossroad at that moment. If the company's standards were not theirs they should not be working there. Of that fact, once brought to light, there was no question. The next step was to look for another company to work for, but there wasn't one that stood out as being the perfect fit, or open their own company on a wing and a prayer, which is what they did. They launched their business in a new direction, focused on special events and met with amazing success. Having the control to try something new, suited to their talents, was a primary factor in their decision to open their own company. They also realized that working for someone in the capacity they were, their earning potential would reach a peak and then remain steady, with very little room for growth. Along with the desire for unlimited authority regarding the type of company they wanted to set up and the direction they wanted to take it, they also wanted financial control by putting themselves in a position where there were no earning limitations.

COSTS AND BENEFITS OF GOING OUT ON YOUR OWN

Going into business for yourself on little more than a wing and a prayer is never recommended, especially for anyone in the event planning field, where events are mapped out with military precision. There are many considerations to look at before taking the leap. Opening your own business can be life affirming and life changing. Such a step may also turn out to be one of the biggest events that you will ever plan—one that can affect your personal and professional life dramatically—and it requires the same visualization, research, development, planning, budget management, attention to detail, skills, timing and logistical considerations that you bring to planning events.

Areas of consideration include:

- Chances for Success
- Personal Character
- Professional Credibility
- Expertise
- Client Base
- Financial Considerations
- Start-Up
- Implementation
- Risk Factors
- Joy Factors

CHANCES FOR SUCCESS

It is important to research the event specialty area you may be contemplating opening a business in. You have to find out who your competitors are, how they market and service their customers, if their companies have grown, and who their target audiences are and who yours would be. As well, knowing how and where you can put yourself in a target-rich environment is another key element on which to base your business plan. Identifying and strategically planning how to meet your business objectives is one of the first steps. Examine the history of those who are already working independently in the field that you want to do business in. Is there anyone else doing exactly what you want to do, and if so, how are they doing?

One event planner did her homework and found that there were very few people working in her market. Her main competitor was doing very well but was in the process of retiring and closing his business. She did not want to offer to buy his business, as the clientele she was going after was very different, but the premise for his business was very similar to what she was about to set up. His clientele had moderate budgets, while she was specializing in doing wrap parties, cast parties, movie premieres, film festival parties, spin-off events and services such as gift selection for very rich individuals in the entertainment and film industries. Instead of buying his company, she bought his knowledge and paid him for showing her the ropes. It was one of the best investments that she could have made. It allowed her to side-step many pitfalls that her competitor had learned only by trial and error, which could have slowed her business down right from the start. The information he shared with her gave her valuable insight into an area that she had no previous experience in. She was running on an idea and was bringing transferable skills to what she was about to undertake. Having the opportunity to learn from someone who was a master in his field prepared her for what to expect. He also briefed her on her legal responsibilities and requirements, and introduced her to lawyers, insurance agents and accountants who were familiar with the industry and who would be available to her if she required their services. The information and industry contacts she received were priceless and gave her a leg up on being successful.

What she did was think outside the box, which was a trait she would need to build and market her business to a clientele whose industries were based on doing exactly that. She knew that if she wanted uncommon success in her chosen field, she would need to be open to pursuing uncommon methods of learning. The creative approach she took to finding out what she needed to know served to help her move forward faster in developing her business. She also displayed that she was not afraid to seek expert advice, find out what she didn't know and ask for help; these were qualities she would need to succeed. She also respected what someone else had to sell. She did not ask for free guidance but paid for professional advice. And that was how she ran her company. She expected to be respected, knew she could not afford to give her services away for free and would not ask that from someone else. Her strong business ethics and her creativity increased her chances for business success.

PERSONAL CHARACTER

What personal characteristics do you possess that would be an asset in running your own company and would require growth? Being self-motivated is essential when you are creating a new business. You must be able to remain excited about the possibilities, remain focused on your goal and be able to continue to move forward when everything is at its most daunting. Above all, you have to be prepared to fight for your success. No one else can do it for you. You have to want it and you have to have courage in your convictions that this is what you want to do. If your normal reaction to facing your fears is retreating to bed and pulling the covers over your head, you must be prepared mentally to move past that and find ways to alleviate your fears.

You cannot afford to sit back when you are launching a new venture. Once you create momentum, it is important to keep it going. To do that you must be self-motivated, continually finding new ways to succeed. If you need a kick-start, there are motivational courses you can take to help inspire you. There are also career coaches who specialize in helping you determine if owning your own business is the right step for you. Remember, not everyone is cut out to be an entrepreneur. Not everyone can be the general and most people should not want to be. You have to listen to your heart and your heart has to be in your business. Your motivation must come from your passion and drive to succeed.

In an established company, it is easy to find motivation. You have a support group around you that is there to encourage you to bring forth your best. If you do not have the funds to hire staff when you are first starting out, often it is just you and the telephone facing the day together. This can be difficult for people that thrive on office interaction and feed off its energy. You have to become the energized force and look for ways that will bring you in contact with like-minded people who share the same thinking and same goals, such as associations for independent event planners. You also need to be able to filter out tempting distractions. They can come in a variety of forms, such as spending hours out of the office looking at office equipment, sales reps calling or dropping by to congratulate you on your new business, starting your workday mid-day and losing precious business contact hours, or sunny days that call out to you to stop what you are doing and take time to play. You know that you are accountable only to you.

If you are starting out working from home—and some very successful businesses have started that way, such as one single mother who grew a multi-million-dollar event planning business out of her basement—there can be family members, television, friends calling to chitchat, housework that calls to you. It is important to establish a working schedule for yourself and others. When you are at the office, you are at the office, and you have to keep that mindset throughout the time you are there. The beauty of working on your own from home is that you can set your own hours, but all play and no work makes Jack and Jackie broke planners. The freedom of choosing when you will do something and how you will do it can be intoxicating in the beginning stages, and you must be able to rein in impulses that will take you away from what you know needs to be done.

Advocates of offices set up in a designated area of their home love the ability of being about to stroll to their office in the middle of the night. Some people find that they at their most creative from 10:00 p.m. till 2:00 a.m., so that is the time they set aside for working on marketing ideas. For others, an early start may be perfect for them to focus on financial matters, so their day begins at 4:00 a.m. With an office located at home, it is important to find a balance between work and home and find the times that work best to complete each task.

You have to look at the impact a home office will have on your personal life and on your business success. For many types of event planning companies, a home office is ideal. In most cases, it is the event planner who goes to the client's office or meets them in a restaurant for a business lunch. Some clients would never think of visiting their event planning company's office, as it would take them away from their day and cost them travel time. Other clients may need to see signs of a professional setting in order for them to consider doing business with your company. It all depends on the type of business you will be doing and what is important to the type of client you are soliciting. Personally and professionally, you have to consider if your business lends itself to being operated out of your home and if it would be the right fit for you. From a professional perspective you have to think about background noises that clients and suppliers will hear over the phone or while meetings are being conducted. For example, babies crying, small children answering the telephone or demanding attention in the middle of a call, kids calling out to each other, dogs barking and lawnmowers whirling can all detract from a professional image.

You also have to contemplate how you feel about suppliers making sales calls at your home or if it would be better to make arrangements, time permitting, to meet them in their offices or a nearby alternatives such as a nearby cafe, hotel or restaurant. On a personal basis, it can be hard on children and family members to be told constantly to be quiet when you are on the telephone and that interrupting you during your workday is not good for business. When you are working from home, you may find that friends and family members feel free to call and chat during workday hours, forgetting that you have to focus on building your business. It will be important to establish boundaries or else personal and professional lines will be crossed.

Working from a home office can sometimes become a part of your persona. One event planning owner used the fact that she worked from home as one of her marketing tools. It was an important part of her public persona and worked to further her business success.

There are many styles of home offices and it is important to find the right fit for you and your business. One creative director owned a farm where he conducted most of his business, and had warehouse space in the city that was zoned for both living and working requirements. The second floor of the warehouse was where he and his staff stored their props and had a reception area. The third floor was combined living and office quarters for overnight stays when he came to the city. Guests were often surprised, after checking in with reception and taking the elevator up to the third floor, to find that the doors opened right into the living room. A desk set up by the elevator doors doubled as reception, but if no one was at the door to greet guests they had to enter on their own into what felt like personal living space, which could make some clients uncomfortable at first. You may be surprised to find some of your clients operating from home as well these days. One corporate executive had a mini-office staffed at home, complete with a personal receptionist and administrative assistant who worked only out of the home office.

In an effort to separate office and living space, one planner converted her garage into an office and left her car parked in the driveway. The garage was insulated and wired, and she had windows installed so she could have natural light to work in. Another planner purchased a duplex and ran his business out of the bottom unit. A home with a separate walkout apartment was the solution for another planner. Clients and suppliers accessed the office via a staircase leading down to the walkout entrance. And a three-story home housed another event planning office. The main floor was the office and the family lived on the upper two floors. A kitchen was installed on the second floor, which also contained the dining room and family room. Bedrooms were located on the third level. In each case, it was important to the individual to have an office setup that would allow him or her to close the door on work at the end of the day and physically leave the office behind. They also wanted office space set up in a manner that allowed them to feel comfortable about having strangers in their personal space.

Other considerations to take into account when considering a home office include making sure that you set up tech support. No longer can you make a call to the IT department. Now you *are* the IT department and you need to make sure that you have good technical advisors just a phone call away. Another area of importance is layout, and if your office space or design will allow you to create workspace for employees as you build your business or need to bring them in on a project basis. As mentioned earlier, one event planning company resolved this dilemma by renting furnished office space from another company, one that gave it access to a boardroom when it needed it, at an extremely reasonable rate. It then hired employees that were capable of working on their own from their own homes and invested money in computers and a good telephone system.

On a personal note, will working from home give you cabin fever? You need to plan time out of the office. Some company owners working from home find having a laptop a necessity in order to give them the flexibility to visit a local cafe and work from there when they need a change of scenery. Others make it a point to get out and go for a walk sometime during their day.

For some, their personal character and the nature of their home life, work and client demands make it essential that they work in an office outside of the home. They look for creative ways to afford a location that will fit their needs when first starting out. For some it may be shared office space or a location that is extremely reasonable through rate or great negotiations. What is most important is knowing what work atmosphere is best for you and for your business. One busy new company owner found that by having a personal driver she was able to work from the backseat of the car and return client calls during her lengthy office commute. For her type of business, it was essential that she locate her office in the city but she refused to live in a concrete jungle. She had small children and wanted to raise them in a more family-friendly atmosphere in the country. Her time sitting in traffic would have been unproductive and this solution worked perfectly for her. Her driver also couriered documents to clients, took her to appointments, ran errands and served as her personal assistant.

For those coming from a work environment that had seemingly a cast of thousands to pitch in at critical times, can you handle the stress when things are down to the wire and there may not be as many available hands or easy access to office equipment that will make the workload easier? Are you comfortable multitasking and taking on different roles? If you grow your company to two or 200 staff members, can you handle the pressure of their dependence on you for their livelihood? What do you have or need to develop as a personal pressure release? For one owner it was having a personal trainer come to the office for an end-of-the-day workout to help him diffuse the day's tensions and relieve anxiety. For another event designer it was ice-skating. For each, it was something they personally found enjoyable and it helped them reconnect with themselves. Also, it was something they could do with their children.

PROFESSIONAL CREDIBILITY

Take stock of what you have done or are doing to build professional credibility that will attract new clients. When you are preparing a client presentation, the product you are now selling is you and your company. What are your positive professional attributes that you are bringing to your company? Do you have letters of personal recommendation for events you have done in the past? Do you have a portfolio of your work? This can be a problem because any pictures from past events that you worked on for another company brings the question of ethics and client confidentiality into play. It may be difficult to get permission to use such photos. What you choose to display and the manner in which it is done will be very revealing about your company's character to new clients. For example, one sales rep for a new event planning company proudly displayed photos of an event that he was claiming his company had done. Unfortunately for him, he was showing the pictures to an event planning supplier who had actually handled the audiovisual component of that event. In fact, some of his own staff members could be seen in the photo background setting up the stage. He knew which event planning company had been contracted to handle the affair and that the new company owner had worked for them in a very minor role. The new event planning company owner was trying to pass off this event as a sample of one of his own and greatly damaged his professional credibility with both those he hoped to do business with and his own sales force.

It is important to prepare how you are going to present yourself to your clients. If you are only at the thinking stages of opening your own company, what can you do now that will serve to highlight your talents and be of value to future clients? To some clients it may be certification, while to others it could be having designed award-winning events. You can't wait until you open your business doors to begin to build a platform from which to launch your business. One newcomer to the hospitality industry was sought after graduation because of graduating with honors, being on the dean's list every year and winning awards by taking part in professional competitions at school. She mastered many areas that related to her chosen field, and along with building a resume she was also building a personal portfolio that would be invaluable to her when she opened her own business. She wanted high marks and practical experience that would bring high regard from the industry and clients. She did not leave work co-op opportunities to chance. She actively pursued companies that were masters in the field she hoped to work in and created co-op opportunities for herself out of the country as what was closer to home would not have the same impact on the specialized career she was seeking. She did the same when she was looking for part-time work and summer jobs. She did not do what was convenient or easy, but instead looked for work in companies that would teach her the skills she would need to run her own business someday and would serve to increase her marketability.

Identify what you have done in the past, what you are doing today and the steps you still need to take to help you establish professional credibility when you go out on your own.

EXPERTISE

It is important to know not only the skills you bring to the table but also what areas of expertise you lack and may require assistance in. If keeping the company books is not your forte then it may be advisable to factor in the costs for hiring an accountant or bookkeeper to help you through the day-to-day stuff. This does not mean that you have to hire a full-time accountant, but budget for these services where and when you need them. Any business needs an accountant, at least for taxes. Every dollar is important when you are running a business and it can be hard to justify spending money on an area that you feel you should be able to manage yourself, but if you are spending your time doing something that someone else could handle rather than freeing you up to take on something that only you are skilled at and you are falling behind on, you have to give it serious consideration. For example, if a new event planning company owner's strength is in creative design and event management with no experience in sales, he may need to bring in expert help in this area as the learning curve could prove to be more costly than bringing a sales rep on board. When money is tight this can be a tough decision to make, but it is important to determine where your time is better spent. If you do decide to bring in sales representatives, how will you be paying them? Will they be receiving a draw against future commissions or working strictly on commission? What terms will be in their contracts?

The transition from entrepreneur working alone and making the commitment to hiring help can be difficult when you are not yet an established, financially stable business. What is important is that you have responsibility for signing the checks and that you are on top and have signed off on all expenditures. As owner you need to know your product, your customer and how you are doing financially. It is not about giving away control but about having access to someone that excels in a field.

The time to build a backup resource of expertise is in the beginning. You cannot wait for a deadline crunch or growth spurt to happen before starting to look for a team of expertise you can bring together to help you through it. It is important to have a list of qualified people at your fingertips who match your business style, who you can count on as company backup in an emergency and who are available on a freelance basis, such as accountants, bookkeepers, lawyers, planning and operations staff, administrative assistance, technical help and staff to handle on-site event orchestration. You can lose business and business opportunities by not preparing in advance to service your clients' needs in busy times and as your company grows.

What will attract industry expertise to your company? Will there be potential for financial or professional growth for sales reps and company employees? As discussed earlier, one employer began giving his main staff—who were essential to the success of his business—shares in the company to encourage them to create a bond with the company and have a vested financial interest in the company's success. The owner also recognized that his employees added tremendously to his company's marketability and that it was in his best interest to make sure that they stayed with the company. The company grew in leaps and bounds thanks in part to the key employees' talents and the owner rewarded them with partnership in his business. Give thought not only to your company's business today but also to its future growth, and look for ways to build, manage and maintain it.

CLIENT BASE

Will you be starting with a client base or will you be starting cold? Is this a business that can be started as a part-time venture—not in conflict with your other work—and one that you can build to become a full-time source of revenue?

One event planning company owner who had been a very successful sales rep got the push she needed to go out on her own when one of her major clients told her that if she opened her own company, he would follow her there. He made good on his promise when she started her business. Is it ethical to take clients with you when you leave a company? The event planning company she worked for had not thought to include a non-compete clause in her contract that would have restricted her ability to solicit its clients for a period of time. She did not make that same mistake when she started hiring sales reps and planning and operations staff to work for her.

Many event planning companies do have non-compete clauses in their sales rep contracts but neglect to impose the same restrictions on their staff hired to design and manage their events, and that leaves the door open for their staff to approach their clients when they open their own companies. And others who have signed non-complete agreements have challenged them in court.

One event planning owner had no problem releasing a client from its contract when it expressed a wish to transfer its business to one of its employees who had started his own company. It did not want to keep the client against its wishes, nor put them in an awkward position, and wanted to have them leave feeling comfortable to return at any time.

You have to go into your business venture with the attitude that you are starting from the ground up unless you are moving into a new area that would not compete with the company you previously worked for. Consideration must be given before taking any actions that would jeopardize your professional reputation and violate business ethics. You would be better served by focusing your energies on identifying new clients, and determining how you can best reach them and sell them on using your services.

FINANCIAL CONSIDERATIONS

Are you prepared financially to be able to handle personal and business expenses until the company is up and running? Will you be in personal financial jeopardy if sales do not come in as fast as expected or if the clients that are booking with you are doing events far in the future?

If finances are tight starting out, it is imperative to come up with a business plan that will allow your focus to be on the company and not on financial survival. It must be specific, not abstract or based on wishful thinking. There are times when expected checks or contracts being signed are delayed, program dates are moved or cancelled in full, and business does not come as quickly as anticipated, and it is imperative that the company be in a position to sustain any unexpected delays.

For many in event planning the focus has been on staying on budget and being creative with the dollars the client has to spend, while meeting objectives and generating return on their investment. When you start your own company, you too have to stay on budget, be creative with the dollars you have to spend, meet your objectives and generate a return on your investment. What you have done in the past and will continue to do for your clients, you must now do for yourself. In order to succeed, you have to be prepared to chase checks, take strong stands on clients adhering to payment schedules and be prepared to walk away from taking on business or continuing to do business with clients that will cost you time, money and resources. You cannot afford to carry someone else's business, as it may end up costing you your own.

When going into business, it is not necessary to have the newest and the best pieces of office equipment, matching office furniture or fully stocked shelves to become successful or to give you a competitive edge. For example, office equipment and furniture, if need be, can be rented, negotiated or borrowed. One very successful event planning company did not have the start-up funds to purchase or even rent an industrial-size photo-copier, and in the beginning any photocopying for presentations was done at the local copy shop (this was before scanning was commonplace). The owners found a workable solution for something they could not afford and invested their money in office essentials and skilled staff that would help them grow. And, until they could afford it, their office furniture was mismatched and beaten up, which they could live with. It was not a reflection on the caliber of events they could create. Very few in the industry could match the results they produced by having some of the industry's best working for them. They were unbeatable, and in due time they not only had matching furniture but owned the building their office was in. They had mastered making the best use of their money, living within their means and making their money work for them.

START-UP

Some event planning companies began with little more than a dream, an area of expertise, a love of what they do, their professional credibility, a mapped-out business and marketing plan, a space designated as "the office," an officially registered company, business name, insurance, installed business telephone lines and fax machine, a business bank account and business checks, letterhead, envelopes, business cards, basic office supplies, limited office equipment, presentation/press kit, a computer, an e-mail address, freelance staff they brought in to help out when and where needed, a courier service and their personal drive and vision. And they have been successful, contracted million-dollar accounts, sought out and collaborated with valuable contacts, and expanded their business.

The Special Events Advisor: A Business and Legal Guide for Event Professionals (John Wiley & Sons, 2003) written by David Sorin, an attorney and event planning consultant, offers business information that event professionals need to start an event planning business and operate it legally. The book covers important topics such as starting an event planning business, buying an event planning business, dealing with partners and shareholders, financing with banks and leasing companies, client service contracts, employee issues, insurance, labor unions, landlord-tenant issues, trucking, intellectual property, accounting, legal liability and exit strategy.

When you are considering company names, look for ones that offer scope. You don't want to be boxed into one area, especially if you have long-term plans to diversify. For example, John Smith & Associates, Jane Smith Productions, The JS Group, J. & J. Corporation, Smith International, J & J Event Consulting, Worldwide Events or Innovative Designs & More may give you more flexibility and room to grow your company than a name that conveys only one aspect of what you do, such as Jack Smith's Table Rentals, Jane Smith's Display or J & J Barbecue Catering. When you go to register your company name, go prepared with several choices. If a search turns up companies with the same name, you will be asked for an alternative on the spot and you want to avoid ending up with a spur-of-the-moment choice that you will come to regret. If applicable, check out the meaning of your company name in other languages. A major car manufacturer had to change the name of its latest model because in French slang it was a rude word. And make sure that the acronym—the word formed by the first initials—of the company name does not spell out something that may be considered offensive.

Event planning, depending on the focus and how the company is being set up, can be done with relatively little setup costs. In an industry where your image reflects your creativity, you can't cut corners on quality when it comes to having your print material professionally designed and created. Some companies are now bringing in copywriters to assist them with their press kits. But you can save dollars on the quantities being ordered when you are starting out. When you are established you can then stock the shelves. The priority in the beginning is capturing the look and feel of your company image. Your marketing materials must make a statement. One event planning company, low on funds but not imagination, did not have the money initially to design the presentation/press kit that best captured the company's creative abilities. The planners did not want to put out a piece that did not reflect the quality of their work and opted instead to produce a series of custom postcards that featured an award-winning event they had done. The postcard worked to serve a dual purpose; they used it as a teaser mailing piece to prospective new clients and as a promotional leave-behind when meeting new clients for the first time.

Perspective is everything. Look at where spending dollars make sense and where it will have the most impact. For example, you can give your company professional polish by using your own domain name as opposed to an ISP address or Web account for your e-mails and website and the cost is not exorbitant yet well worth the return in company representation. The same applies with regard to telephone lines. For anyone considering setting up an office from home, adding an extra residential line is not an option—you must have a business line. If you are placing yourself in the path of business, your target must be able to find your listing in a business directory. Also, give careful consideration regarding how many lines or cables you will need to operate your business telephones, faxes and computers. In busy times will you be able to operate at full speed or will you experience delays if you don't have sufficient lines installed? Also be sure to buy equipment that can meet your business needs and handle volume—equipment that is geared to personal home use will not stand up to heavy use.

	It is always a good idea to have a simple backup telephone that you can purchase at a local hardware store. When major blackouts occurred in North America, with some areas having no electricity for up to a week, cell phones and sophisticated telephone systems were not able to operate and the only telephones that were working were the old-fashioned type that plugged directly into the telephone jack without requiring an electrical outlet.

IMPLEMENTATION

Planners who use the event planning principles of visualization can prepare themselves for what lies ahead. Visualization helps you to uncover business blind spots and address them in advance. This is the time to look at the big picture of everything that running your own event planning business could entail. Just as event planning is based on two distinct sides, creative and logistics, so is running your own event planning business. There is the creative side, which now is expanded to include marketing, and the logistical side, which covers event operations and what you need to put in place to run a successful business. Thought must be given to how and who will be responsible for handling each specific area, such as:

Administrative

- Who will answer the office telephone?
- What type of telephone system will best meet my needs?
- How many telephone lines will I require?
- Who will open, sort, date stamp and distribute mail?
- Who will be responsible for office cleaning?
- Who will be in charge of maintaining control of office supplies and re-orders?
- Who will set up business accounts for couriers, office supplies, telephone service, etc?

- Who will set up and maintain the filing system for the office for incoming material and dead files?
- Who will administrative staff report to?

Qualifying Potential Clients

- Who will solicit clients and make sales calls?
- Where will they be doing it from? From the office? From home?
- What will they require in order for them to do their job? Letterhead, envelopes, presentation kits, someone to prepare their sales letters, postage, courier service, access to long distance?
- What office equipment will they require? A desk, chair, telephone, computer, printer, scanner, photocopier, fax machine, basic office supplies?
- How will they be compensated?
- What business expenses could they incur that could be classified as office expenses? Parking, mileage, business lunches?
- Who will provide sales training?
- Who will sales representatives report to?

Researching and Developing Client Proposals

- Who will be responsible for researching, developing and preparing client proposals?
- What other responsibilities will they have?
- Where will they operate from? From the office? From home?
- What will they require in order for them to prepare the proposals? Letterhead, envelopes, proposal folders, someone to prepare their proposals (or will they handle own typing), courier service, access to long distance?
- What office equipment will they require? A desk, chair, telephone, computer, printer, scanner, photocopier, fax machine, calculator, basic office supplies?
- What level of skill do they have? Will expert assistance need to be brought in?
- How many requests for proposals can the office handle?

- Who will review their proposals against supplier quotes to make sure that costs are correct and that nothing has been overlooked?
- What business expenses could they incur that could be classified as office expenses? Parking, mileage, familiarization trips, site inspections?
- Who will the planning staff report to?

Client Presentations

- Who will head up client presentations?
- Will anyone else from the office be required to accompany them, pulling them away from day-to-day deadlines or office responsibilities?
- Will a laptop or anything else be required for presentations?

Doing Program Recostings

- Who will do any client proposal recostings?
- How many recostings will staff be capable of handling per month in addition to their other responsibilities?
- Do I have fully trained people I can bring in to help in crunch-time periods so that I do not lose any business opportunities?

Contracting

- Who will be responsible for preparing client contracts?
- Do I have a lawyer, familiar with event planning requirements, that can draw up a boilerplate contract and review final contract additions and requested deletions?
- Who will have signing authority for client contracts?

Event Management

- How will event operations and management be handled? Will the person who designed the event be responsible for event management as well, or will the file be passed on to someone who specializes in event planning?
- What skills do they possess that qualify them for this position?

- Will any expertise be required in this area?

- What office equipment will they require?

- How many event operation files can they handle at the same time?

- Who will handle packaging and distribution of any client promotional material?

- Who will ensure that payment schedules are adhered to?

- Will there be times that I need to bring someone in to help?

- Will this person be required to travel out of the office for client meetings, site inspections, advancing the event, conducting pre-event meetings with suppliers or to oversee the event?

- How will their being out of the office affect other client deadlines?

- Who will operations staff report to?

On-Site Orchestration

- Who will be traveling in advance to oversee move-in and setup?

- Who will be handling on-site orchestration?

- What on-site equipment could be required? Cell phones, laptops, trucking?

- What freelance event directors do I have access to?

- Who will be responsible for signing off on any supplier charges and billing?

- Who will on-site staff report to?

Event Reconciliation

- Who will handle event reconciliation?

- Who will review event reconciliation before it goes to the client?

Event Evaluation

- Who will conduct the event evaluation with the client, supplier and the office?

Marketing and Promotional Material

- Who will research company print material options? Letterhead, envelopes, presentation/press kits?
- Who will handle business development?
- Who will identify the competition?
- Who will research what the competition is doing?
- Who will determine how my company can set itself apart from the competition?
- Who will look at the feasibility of creating niche markets, spin-off business, diversification?
- Who will be responsible for looking for marketing opportunities?
- Who will head up marketing campaigns?
- Who will the person in charge of marketing and promotional material report to?

Accounting

- Who will handle accounting?
- Who will pay the bills?
- Who will set up an accounting system?
- Who will monitor cash flow?
- Who will look for investment opportunities?
- Who will do the daily banking?
- Who will monitor and maintain petty cash?
- Who will research and determine the best telephone company, Internet provider, bank, types of bank accounts, and decide on the look of company checks, which office equipment to purchase or rent, etc.?

Legal Matters

- Who will be the company's signing officers?
- Who will be ensuring that all legal requirements, permits and insurance are in place?

- Who will fill out the actual forms?
- Who will oversee employee benefits, contracts, etc.?
- Who will issue employee paychecks?

Education and Training of Staff

- Who will be in charge of hiring staff?
- Who will train and motivate staff?
- Who will handle human resources?
- Who will evaluate staff?
- Who will handle office politics?

If the answer to all of the above is you, then you have to devise a master plan to be able to prioritize your time, determine how you will invest your money and identify red flag areas where you are going to need help. All of these areas can demand your attention in a day—every day—as can personal life issues with family and friends. How will you need to structure your office? Structure your day? It can be a juggling act when you are first starting out. If you are operating your business on your own with only the help of occasional staff, there is the very real problem of overload and creating a situation that puts your business success at risk. If you are out selling to clients, you are not working on files, and if you are immersed in event operations, you are not selling or marketing your company. When the event ends, what then? What if you have not put anything in place to go forward? You will then find yourself in a mad scramble to find your next event. What if you have a client that requires extra attention and handholding? Will you be able to handle that? One event planner who opened his own business found himself in that position and he ended up firing his client—because he just could not manage their nonstop phone calls from 7:00 a.m. till midnight. In the beginning, anxious to please, he did not put business boundaries in place and he set a precedent that it was acceptable to call when they pleased and he would be there to answer their questions and make repeated changes to their program. He had not structured his management fee to cover this contingency. Ways that he could have protected himself from underpricing his services are outlined in detail in my book *The*

Business of Event Planning: Behind-the-Scenes Secrets of Successful Special Events (John Wiley & Sons, 2002). Setting up and running your company will require using your entire event planning training expertise, just applied in differently ways. This training is an added business bonus that some people opening their own companies in other industries do not have.

Some people in the hospitality and event planning industry experienced great success by creating a business out of two things they love and specializing in one of these areas, creating their niche. There was still room for growth and diversification in their choices but their focus was concentrated on what they knew and did best, and they grew their businesses from that starting point. Had they tried to be everything to their clients in an area they knew nothing about and handled business demands on top of that, they could easily have been overwhelmed. One caterer who kept her focus on providing excellent catering service with creative menu planning was eventually able to expand her business and open a restaurant that was frequented by her clients. Someone else did it in reverse; she started by operating a specialty food store and catering demands grew from that. A very successful business was created by one entrepreneur's love of scuba diving and photography— he became a master of underwater photography and was in great demand. Another created her business out of her combined passion for baking and flowers, and created breathtaking cakes that were sought after by event planners around the world.

How you are going to accomplish what you are setting out to do must be laid out before you begin. Just as you would never go into an event without being fully prepared, don't venture into opening your own business without giving thought to what needs to be done to ensure your success.

RISK FACTORS

There are very real risks, personal and professional, to opening your own company. The best-case scenario is that you are doing something you love, in a way you love, and are successful. The worst-case scenario is that you go back to working for someone else but doing it differently, knowing exactly what will be required to bring you job and personal satisfaction. In both cases, you will experience a range of emotions, from feeling battered, bruised and exhausted to feeling unbelievable energy and exhilaration—often occurring on the same day—from having challenged yourself to follow your dream. Sometimes in life, the greatest risk you can take is to do nothing at all.

Some risks you may encounter and questions you may find yourself asking include:

Financial Risks

- Will I have enough money to meet business expenses?
- Will I have enough money to repair or replace equipment as needed?
- What happens if there is no return on investment?

Professional Risks

- What happens if I fail?
- Will I be able to find work again in the industry if this doesn't work out?
- Will I still have time to keep myself current with everything else I am juggling?

Personal Risks

- Can my family handle not having a guaranteed paycheck coming in every two weeks?
- Will my relationships suffer due to the time I need to invest getting my company running?
- Can I fight my fears and have the courage to keep going forward?

Having a large office will not ensure success or take away risk. Neither will having a fully staffed office or start-up funds. One company started in a 400-square-foot studio apartment with only a single person. It began with just one product to sell, but it was a unique product. Today it's a multi-million-dollar company. The planner did not put himself at risk by spending funds he did not have on office space. He invested in marketing and in his website and spent his money where it would do the most good. It is not about how shiny an office you have or how many toys. It is about having an idea you are passionate about, using your creativity to find a way to make it work and managing the risk so that you place yourself in a position of meeting your objectives. The process follows the same event planning principles that planners use to help their clients succeed.

Learn from those who have gone before you. If you are ever in Disney World or Disneyland, look for a card in the gift shop that simply says, "It all began with a mouse"—and stop for a moment to take in exactly where and what that led to.

Joy Factors

There is an event in a ropes course where the challenge is to climb a telephone pole, stand on top and jump off (a sample ropes course can be found at www.miravalresort.com). Participants are outfitted with protective gear such as helmets, harnesses, belay devices and carabiners to ensure their safety. There are people manning the ropes, on belay, to lower climbers safely to the ground. They are at the ready to assist climbers by giving or taking away slack as needed. As climbers set out to climb the pole, some are stricken with fear and cling to the pole for all they are worth, afraid to take one more step, while others climb the pole with ease and then fight with their internal fears about taking that final step to the top. Still others take measured steps, climb with confidence to the top and stand triumphant, thrilled with what they achieved, and fling themselves forward into the unknown with joyous abandon. The built-in risks of climbing the pole are both real and perceived. Whether you climb halfway up the telephone pole, make it further up or stand aloft, you are coming down in the same fashion—with those on belay lowering you safely to the ground. The real test is not in how far you climb up the pole or if you even jump off it, but in taking just one step more—whatever that may be—than you are comfortable with. If you can do that, you will feel true joy in your accomplishments. When you open your own business, the experience can be similar to the rope experience. Some of your fears will be real and some perceived. There will be times when you may be clinging to the side of the pole, wondering whatever possessed you to take on something like this, and there will be other times when you climb right up with no hesitation in your step. There will be people you will encounter that will give you slack and take up your slack.

However, doing what you love in a manner that is meaningful to you can bring joy into your personal and professional life. It will require you to take steps every day that may take you out of your comfort zone, but the key to remember is with each step you take that takes you forward past your fears, you will experience pleasure of having grown.

There are many joys in owning your own business, and these can include:

- The joy of having a vision and making it a reality
- The joy of being able to do something that you are passionate about
- The joy of having more control of your destiny
- The joy of personal and professional independence
- The joy of financial freedom
- The joy of being able to grow your company in the direction that matters most to you
- The joy of being able to set your own pace and move forward at a speed that works for you
- The joy of challenging yourself to do something you love

Some people come out of the experience of having had their own business being at peace with returning to the workforce and working for another company. For them, being a business owner was not the right fit, but they take away an amazing new set of skills and they come out of the experience knowing the type of company they would be the perfect fit for. What they have to prepare for, though, is people questioning their decision to return to working for someone else. Some companies are fearful of hiring those who have shown that they have an entrepreneurial side, fearing that if they invest in them they may leave to take off on a new venture. Other people thrive on having their own business, and for them there is no turning back. They are driven to succeed and will not stop until they do.

What is important is to know when what you are doing does not feel right and to listen to your internal dialogue. Some stay too long in work situations where they are unhappy and afraid to make a move, or hang on to their company when it no longer brings them joy. One key to success is knowing when to let go, when to move forward and where you need to challenge yourself to take one step more than you are comfortable with, whether you are working for someone else or yourself.

Questions to ask when you are considering whether or not to go into business for yourself include:

- Do I have the courage and conviction to make this move?
- Have I done all I can to prepare for this?
- Can I handle financial ups and downs—emotionally and from a business and personal perspective?
- Do I have senior counsel I can turn to for advice?
- Can I lead a team to believe in my dream?
- Do I believe in what I have to offer?
- What are my strengths?
- Can I identify areas I will need help in?
- What am I risking by moving forward?
- What am I risking if I don't (e.g., I should've, I could've, if only I would've...)?
- Can I sell myself?
- Can I sell what I have to offer?
- Can I create a business that has "legs" and provides growth opportunities?
- How will I market myself?
- How will I market my business?
- What expert help will I need to bring in?
- Do I know where I am best investing my money?
- Have I visualized exactly what I will need to succeed?
- Have I researched all options?
- Have I developed my plan?
- Do I know what I need to manage my business?
- Do I have the skills and ability to implement all that I need to?

CONCLUSION

In a world where competition is stronger than ever, it is essential to give yourself the gift of self-investment that will serve to increase your marketability whether you work for somebody else or for yourself. Circumstances can change overnight and it is important to be prepared to meet new challenges. If you use all your time to invest in only doing your job—not in growing yourself—you could be left high and dry when market conditions change. There is value in developing take-away tools that will serve you wherever you go, whatever you do. Do not limit your personal and professional life by not building your marketability to its fullest. Acquire areas of expertise in your personal passions as well as those that have professional merit and that can advance you in business. Being left behind on the sidelines of life and business is a choice and it can affect your future. The event planning industry offers a wealth of resources and opportunities that will take you far—explore them. Use your areas of expertise to create your niche in the event planning world. Use your talents as a marketing tool in order to stand out from your competition. This will be of benefit to you personally and professionally. Adding layers of marketability has great worth.

Master market development. Defining your business objectives will lead you to identifying who your client truly is. Once you can pinpoint your client, you can target your talents to better meet their needs. This exercise will also enable you to discover where your areas of strength and weakness are in your chosen field. It will clearly tell you what you need to know and what your next steps should be. It will help you to map out a plan of action that will allow you to develop your market and your talents to their maximum.

Learn to detect target-rich environments in which to pursue your marketing endeavors. Remember not to plant marketing seeds in sand; you are in search of rich soil so that what you plant will take root, flourish and grow. Targeting your marketing to your specific audience will increase your chances for a positive response. Be creative in your approach. Some clients turn to the event planning industry to help them motivate and inspire their participants, while others look to have their guests dazzled and delighted. In either case, meeting their objectives will be based on a foundation of creativity. That creativity must be reflected in not only your proposals but also in how you present yourself personally and professionally. If you are soliciting sales, do it with flair. It is difficult to tell clients how creative you are if what you present before them is mediocrity. Each client you present to needs to be approached in a manner that speaks to their industry or personal concerns and addresses them in a language they relate to. Sell them on your being their event planning solution.

Look for ways to diversify as an individual and as a company so that you can create diverse streams of income. Plan with the unknown in mind and be prepared to switch gears at a moment's notice. We know now how quickly the industry can be shaken up, and if you want to thrive, not merely survive, in the industry you cannot afford to become complacent. Remember the ABCs of event planning discussed in *Event Planning Ethics and Etiquette*. Plan A is anticipation, Plan B is backup and Plan C is moving into crisis management mode. Today it is imperative not only to have Plan B at the ready, but to put Plan B in effect and have Plan C ready to go the minute the next headline flashes around the world that could affect the event planning industry, your professional earning potential and your personal savings. Use the event planning techniques you know:

- Sales
- Marketing
- Business development
- Visualization
- Research
- Development
- Planning
- Management/operations
- Execution/implementation

Master the principles that lead to producing successful events and then adopt, adapt and apply them to marketing yourself as the product personally and professionally. Using these same principles and combining them with your creative vision will help you decide when and if you should go out on your own, and regardless of your decision, how to gain the competitive edge in marketing your event planning business.

APPENDIX A

Leading Internationally Recognized Industry Certifications

Certification and qualification processes are subject to change.

CEM—CERTIFIED IN EXHIBITION MANAGEMENT

CEM is an exhibit industry professional designated by the International Association for Exhibition Management (IAEM).

CERTIFICATION ELIGIBILITY

- No educational requirements
- Three years of active involvement in the industry
- Successful completion of all nine parts, including passing the appropriate examinations within three years beginning the year following the first pass

QUALIFICATION PROCESS

The CEM Learning Program requires that a participant complete a nine-part education program, consisting of seven mandatory courses and two elective courses. The courses are offered in three different learning environments:

- On location—a one-day program, followed immediately by an examination
- Online—a four-week facilitated Web-based course
- Self-paced (elective courses only)

For information and to register, contact IAEM (www.iaem.org).

CITE—CERTIFIED INCENTIVE TRAVEL EXECUTIVE

Earning the CITE mark of distinction will help set incentive planners apart from other incentive travel practitioners. Those attaining a CITE certification demonstrate their extensive knowledge of the industry by achieving its highest standard of excellence.

CERTIFICATION ELIGIBILITY

- Membership in SITE (The Society of Incentive & Travel Executives)
- Achievement of 100 points for a combination of industry experience and activities in SITE according to its Point Qualification Chart
- Payment of the application fee

QUALIFICATION PROCESS

- Choose a mentor—this person must a SITE member and a CITE
- Successfully completion of the three-hour written examination covering the following aspects of an incentive travel program: Funding the Program; Qualification; Finance/Budgeting; Destination Selection; Marketing/Promotion; Transportation; Accommodations; DMC/Event Company/Ground Operator; and Ethics (you will be given a Study Guide to assist you in your preparation)
- Choose a topic for your research paper and submit an outline for approval
- Prepare a 3,000-word original thesis with bibliography

For information and to register, contact SITE (www.site-intl.org).

CME—CERTIFIED MANAGER OF EXHIBITS

The Certified Manager of Exhibits (CME) is the only association-sponsored certification program that recognizes professionalism in exhibit management and marketing. It is designated by the Trade Show Exhibitors Association (TSEA).

CERTIFICATION ELIGIBILITY

* On-the-job experience

QUALIFICATION PROCESS

* Minimum of seven CEU (Continuing Education Units) points (one CEU equals 10 hours; programs offered through TSEA count as double points)
* Letter of reference from your employer
* Critical analysis—case study essay

    For information and to register, contact TSEA (www.tsea.org).

CMM—GLOBAL CERTIFICATION IN MEETING MANAGEMENT

The Global CMM program includes five days of intensive training as well as a post-residency business project and an examination. It is offered by Meeting Professionals International (MPI), and is a complement to the CMP designation offered by the Convention Industry Council (CIC).

CERTIFICATION ELIGIBILITY

To determine eligibility for the CMM program you must complete the online CMM application and submit the nonrefundable application (different application fees for MPI members/non-members).

    The application asks for your:

* Industry certifications
* Formal education
* Professional education

- Professional experience
- International experience/global skills
- Professional contributions
- Additional/exceptional qualifications (including references)

QUALIFICATION PROCESS

The Global CMM program is a comprehensive, strategic program that requires commitment and dedication to reach the goal. It entails:

- A detailed application to determine eligibility
- Pre-residency assignments, including involvement in a small group through technology, as well as pre-reading
- A four half-day residential, full-immersion course with top-level faculty
- Continuation of the small group work on a case study while in-residence
- An examination, taken either on your own personal laptop before departure, or within one week following the residency online on the MPI website
- A post-residency business project due six weeks following the residency aspect

    Online courses are also available.
    For information and to register, contact: MPI (www.mpiweb.org).

CMP—CERTIFIED MEETING PROFESSIONAL

CMP certifies competency in 25 areas of meeting management designated by the Convention Industry Council (CIC). This internationally recognized certification program that evaluates the competency of meeting professionals. The CMP designation represents the standard of excellence in today's meeting and exposition industry.

CERTIFICATION ELIGIBILITY

- Four-year university degree with a major in meeting and convention management, or a minimum of three years of experience in meeting management
- Currently employed in a meeting management capacity
- Responsible and accountable for the successful completion of meetings

QUALIFICATION PROCESS

- The certification program requires a two-step process in which applicants 1) demonstrate via a point system their broad range of experience in the field of meeting management and 2) successfully complete a written examination covering the functions performed in meeting management
- Eligibility to be seated for the CMP exam is based on a system whereby the applicant accrues points derived from actual experience in several aspects of meeting management. To qualify as an applicant, an individual must acquire a minimum of 90 out of 150 possible points. Points are assigned within five specific areas of meeting management:
  - Experience in meeting management
  - Management responsibility
  - Education and continuing education
  - Membership in professional organizations
  - Professional contribution to the field

For information and to register, contact CIC (www.conventionindustry.org).

Information can also be obtained through MPI (www.mpiweb.org).

CSEP—CERTIFIED SPECIAL EVENTS PROFESSIONAL

The CSEP designation is earned through education, performance, experience, and service to the industry, and reflects a commitment to professional conduct and ethics. It is awarded by the International Special Events Society (ISES) and its Certification Committee.

CERTIFICATION ELIGIBILITY

- Enroll and accumulate points through experience and service
- Begin a self-study program or start a study group
- Demonstrate ability to create, cultivate, design, implement, produce, and recap a special event

QUALIFICATION PROCESS

- Enrollment in CSEP program
- Accumulation of 35 points through industry experience and leadership, education and service
- Application to take the CSEP exam, which is in three parts: 1) essay—a case study in which the exam candidate demonstrates his/her mastery of the required competencies; 2) objective— based on the glossary of terms; and 3) portfolio assessment
- Successful completion of the exam

  For information and to register, contact ISES (www.ises.com).

Special Note:
The well-known George Washington University Event Management Certificate Course is now being offered throughout the world in a consortium of schools (thirteen in total around the world, with Ryerson University being the only one in Canada). The George Washington University Ryerson Event Management Certificate enables students to build qualifying points to sit the SEP examination and obtain the CSEP. Distance learning is available.

APPENDIX B

Industry Associations and Councils

Here are sample industry associations and councils, many of which have chapters worldwide.

CIC—CONVENTION INDUSTRY COUNCIL

This umbrella group for the trade show industry runs the Certified Meeting Professional (CMP) and Accepted Practices Exchange programs.

Website: www.conventionindustry.org

CSES—CANADIAN SPECIAL EVENTS SOCIETY

CSES is a Canadian association representing the special events industry in Canada.

Website: www.cses.ca

HSMAI—HOTEL SALES AND MARKETING ASSOCIATION INTERNATIONAL

HSMAI is a global organization of sales and marketing professionals representing all segments of the hospitality industry.

Website: www.hsmai.com

IAAP—INTERNATIONAL ASSOCIATION OF ADMINISTRATIVE PROFESSIONALS

IAAP is the world's largest association for administrative support staff.

Website: www.iaap-hq.org

IACC—INTERNATIONAL ASSOCIATION OF CONFERENCE CENTERS NORTH AMERICA

IACC is a not-for-profit, facilities-based organization founded to promote a greater awareness and understanding of the unique features of conference centers around the world.

Website: www.iaccnorthamerica.org

IAEM—INTERNATIONAL ASSOCIATION FOR EXHIBITION MANAGEMENT

IAEM is one of the premier associations for all individuals with business interests in the exhibition industry.

Website: www.iaem.org

IMPAC—INDEPENDENT MEETING PLANNERS ASSOCIATION OF CANADA, INC.

IMPAC is dedicated to providing resources, education and networking opportunities to independent meeting planners.

Website: www.impaccanada.com

ISES—INTERNATIONAL SPECIAL EVENTS SOCIETY

The mission of ISES is to educate, advance and promote the special events industry and its network of professionals, along with related industries.

Website: www.ises.com

MPI—MEETING PROFESSIONALS INTERNATIONAL

MPI is the meeting industry's premier educational, technological and networking resource organization.

Website: www.mpiweb.org

NACE—NATIONAL ASSOCIATION OF CATERING EXECUTIVES

NACE serves hotels and off-premise and on-premise caterers, providing top-quality educational and networking opportunities and affiliate vendor interaction.

Website: www.nace.net

PCMA—PROFESSIONAL CONVENTION MANAGEMENT ASSOCIATION

PCMA is a nonprofit international association of professionals in the meetings industry whose mission is to deliver breakthrough education and promote the value of professional convention management.

Website: www.pcma.org

SCMP—SOCIETY OF CORPORATE MEETING PLANNERS

SCMP membership consists of corporate meeting professionals and convention/service professionals. SCMP exists to further industry education and promote professionalism in the corporate meeting arena.

Website: www.scmp.org

SITE—SOCIETY OF INCENTIVE & TRAVEL EXECUTIVES

SITE is a worldwide organization of business professionals dedicated to the recognition and development of motivational and performance improvement strategies of which travel is a key component. It recognizes the global cultural difference and practices in developing these strategies, and serves as a prime networking and educational opportunity for its members.

Website: www.site-intl.org

APPENDIX C

Industry Magazines, Books, Online Publications and Resources

Amazon:
www.amazon.com (worldwide) or www.amazon.ca (Canada);
search event planning

Barnes and Noble:
www.barnesandnoble.com (United States);
search event planning

BiZBash: www.bizbash.com

Canadian Event Perspective magazine:
www.canadianspecialevents.com

Canadian Events Suppliers Guide:
www.canadianspecialevents.com

Chapters Indigo:
www.chapters.indigo.ca (Canada)

Charity Village (non-profit):
www.charityvillage.com

Conventions Meetings Canada Directory:
www.bizlink.com/cmc.htm

Corporate and Incentive Travel magazine:
www.corporate-inc-travel.com

Corporate Meetings and Incentives:
www.corpmeetings.net

Event Solutions magazine:
www.event-solutions.com

Incentive magazine:
www.incentivemag.com

Insurance Conference Planner:
www.icplanner.com

Marketing Magazine:
www.marketingmag.ca

Medical Meetings:
www.medicalmeetings.net

MeetingNews:
www.meetingnews.com

Meetings and Incentive Travel magazine:
www.meetingscanada.com

MeetingsNet:
www.meetingsnet.com

MIMlist:
www.mim.com

MPI online bookstore:
www.mpiweb.org/resources/bookstore/

PR Canada:
www.prcanada.ca

Special Events magazine:
www.specialevents.com

Successful Meetings magazine:
www.successmtgs.com

The Meeting Professional magazine:
www.mpiweb.org/news/tmp/

APPENDIX D

Industry Conferences, Congresses, Trade Shows and Award Shows

BiZBash The Fresh Idea Show:
www.bizbash.com

Canadian Event Industry Awards (CEIA):
www.canadianspecialevents.com

Canadian Meeting & Incentive Travel Symposium & Trade Show (CMITS):
www.meetingscanada.com

CEP Special Events & Meetings Expo (CSEME):
www.canadianspecialevents.com

EIBTM Exhibition (meetings and incentive industry):
www.eibtm.ch

Events and Travel Services Shows:
www.meetingscanada.com

IMEX Worldwide Exhibition for Incentive Travel, Meetings and Events:
www.imex-frankfurt.com

MPI Professional Education Conference and World Education Congress:
www.mpiweb.org

SITE Crystal Awards:
www.site-intl.org or www.motivationshow.com

SITE International Conference:
www.site-intl.org

The Motivation Show:
www.motivationshow.com

The Special Event Show:
www.thespecialeventshow.com

World Travel Market (incentives):
www.worldtravelmart.co.uk

APPENDIX E

Sample Creative Concepts

Here are creative concept examples for a corporate event (Sample A), a fundraising gala (Sample B) and a theme event (Sample C—one theme with two different creative concepts). Note that there is no "tone" of language that's right for every client or concept. Tailor your language to appeal to each individual situation.

SAMPLE A: CONCEPT FOR CORPORATE EVENT

THE EVENT

New car product launch and company appreciation dinner for a car manufacturer. Theme to tie in with company objective of being a leader in its industry—in performance and safety—leading the way to the future. Its new cars to be revealed and showcased in the room.

THE THEME

Wheels of Change/Evolution by Design

Inukshuk

For centuries, massive stone figures built in the image of a human have stood silhouetted on the treeless Arctic horizons. They are called Inukshuk, erected by the Inuit people. One of their functions was to serve as guides, giving direction to fellow travelers and to all who would follow. They were a practical method of pointing to the passage found to be better and safer. In this purpose, they stand today, symbols of our responsibility to one another and our dependence on one another. The Inukshuk figure is a meaningful, powerful symbol of the importance of making an effort today—doing something, saying something, giving something—that will make the way better and safer for all of us tomorrow.

The Inukshuk Figure

A quiet, compelling, powerful communication given to acknowledge a person or a group that has shown leadership and direction in a meaningful way. It recognizes integrity of vision and responsible action of a company towards its people and the world around us. It represents, communicates and reminds us of the importance of the higher values common to all of us.

THE SETTING

The doors open. The room is bathed in darkness, completely draped from ceiling to floor in black. Steam rises from the floor, creating an atmosphere of the stillness and the mists of the Arctic tundra. Twinkling everywhere against the black are hundreds of white lights, symbolic of the majestic northern lights. Lasers flash upon 15-foot Inuit stone sculptures standing guard over the night, and the new cars are positioned by their base. The sound of a drum echoes in the darkness.

Tables are snowy white, accented with icy white neon and tones of icy blue. Each napkin is tied with icicle napkin rings and in the center of each table will be a circlet of small Inukshuk figures around glowing blue candlelight. At the end of the evening, each guest will take home an Inukshuk figure as a memento of the night and a reminder of the power inherent in their ability to guide others.

The dinner will be a delicious sampling of native offerings, beautifully presented and elegantly served. When coffee and liqueurs have been served, a pool of blue light will appear on stage and the voiceover will introduce Inuit singer Susan Aglukark for a private performance. A chorus of children's voices will be heard around the room. The children will enter from the back of the room and make their way to the stage. Susan Aglukark's music touches on "wheels of change," how we are "all family" and how she is now "singing her dreams" and resonates that together we can make all of our dreams come true. Guests are carried back to the meaning of this evening's symbol—the Inukshuk and how it stands as a directional marker guiding the way, symbolic of our responsibility to one another, our dependence on one another—and the importance of making an effort today—doing something, saying something, giving something—that will make the way better and safer for all of us tomorrow. The performance will also include Inuit dancers and drummers.

THE INVITATION

Custom invitations that incorporate a description and image of the Inukshuk and the meaning behind the statue as it ties into tonight's theme. Custom menus will also carry the theme.

THE DECOR

Inukshuk figures around the room.

Two Inukshuk figures set to each side of the entrance that will become platforms for two drummers.

Further treatment at each Inukshuk location to include blue mini-lights and acrylic shards for shattered ice effect.

Indoor pyrotechnics to simulate cascade of snow falling as the doors open.

Snow blanket for base of Inukshuk figures. Foam snowballs.

Floor-to-ceiling black drape with stars and simulated northern lights effect.

Bar areas—"glass block" bars enhanced with blue lights.

Fiber-optic shimmer curtain for stage area with "iceberg" stage set. Stage for announcement and for high-energy dance band to follow private performance.

Center revolving stage for performance, creating a "theater in the round" atmosphere.

Wall of ice lit with blue lights. Theme could be carved into ice block.

Laser show. Dramatic lighting and special effects that will highlight the cars positioned around the room.

TABLE TREATMENTS

Combination of neon table treatments to include:

Full circle neon table tops with cloths placed over the neon piece to diffuse the light.

Neon pedestals high as base for florals (white on white) or smaller Inukshuks.

White-on-white linens.

Pale ice blue napkins with icicle and ribbon accent.

Randomly strewn acrylic "ice cubes" in various stages.

Glass block pedestals for florals set on full neon tabletops.

White chaircovers with silver or pale blue ties.

Cobalt blue glassware and plates.

PLACE CARDS

An engraved compass with each guest's name will be used as a place card (tying in with theme—direction/leading the way).

THE MENU

Butternut Squash Soup (with a trail of roasted pumpkinseeds laid across the top)

Choice of:
Grilled Salmon with Rose Hip Sauce and Smoked Oyster Potato Cakes

Roasted Turkey with Cranberry Pinion Sauce

Buffalo Brisket Barbecue with Grilled Corn, Chili Oil and Pico de Gallo

Venison and Ribbons of Summer Squash with Sage Pesto

Custom-Baked Miniature Alaskas

Plates will be dusted with paprika–in the pattern of directional markings—north, east, south and west—and set upon juniper or pine branches.

TAKE-AWAY GIFT

Autographed Susan Aglukark CD.

OPTIONAL ENHANCEMENT

Through Star Registry, naming an actual star after the company's stars.

Existing lights can be changed to icicle light fixtures.

SAMPLE B: CONCEPT FOR A FUNDRAISING EVENT

THE EVENT

An upscale evening fundraiser. Many of the invited guests would be business leaders in the financial industry.

THE THEME

Parade of the Big Bottles—Wine Auction Gala Fundraiser.

THE SETTING

The ideal setting for a wine auction would be in a tent in a glen or vineyard. The main tent would need to accommodate dinner and dancing. A separate or adjoining tent could be used to house the reception and silent auction items.

Inside the tent (or ballroom) you would want to recreate either the feeling of being in an actual vineyard or reproduce the ambiance of an event at a private winery in Napa, complete with candelabras, splashing fountains, classical background music and specialty lighting. Minivignettes can be created around the room and pinspot lighting will help to create dramatic effects. If you are holding your event in a ballroom, you can replicate the feeling of being in a tent by using draping and/or actual tent liners.

INVITATION OPTIONS

Mock oversize wine label invitations.

Paper invitations with actual wine cork attached to the invitation or halved and adhered to the invitation.

Wine bottles with custom-printed theme labels. The formal invitation can be rolled and placed inside the bottle.

Etched bottles of wine. The bottle design can feature your theme logo. The formal invitation can be imprinted and inserted into the bottle and corked, or if the bottle is being sent filled, attached to the neck of the bottle with grapevine.

SILENT AUCTION RECEPTION

Serve select wines (limited or full section) and/or champagne paired with hors d'oeuvres that will allow for flavor compatibility. Offering full bar service is not recommended for a wine-themed event. Keep the focus on wine and limit your choices to wine and/or champagne along with non-alcoholic beverages and an assortment of mineral waters.

SAMPLE PAIRINGS—SIPPING AND SAMPLING

When Serving:	Passed Hors D'oeuvres Selection Could Include:
Sparkling Wine	Jumbo Shrimp (or Crab Claws) Salmon Tartar Foie Gras
Sauvignon Blanc	Smoke Salmon Mousse Pork, Shrimp Combination Vegetable Fritters (e.g., Artichoke and Asparagus)

Chardonnay	Seared Tuna Crab Fritters Chicken Satay with Peanut Sauce
Pinot Noir	Smoked Duck Breast with Melon Oysters on the Half Shell with Hollandaise Phyllo Pastry with Goat Cheese
Merlot	Brie Beef Satay with Teriyaki Duck with Hoisin Sauce
Cabernet Sauvignon	Roquefort Paired with Apple Beef Carpaccio Baby Lamb Chops
Champagne	Caviar on Ice (Beluga, Sevruga or Osetra) Blini with Crème Fraiche, Sour Cream Chopped Egg White, Egg Yolk, Parsley and Lemon

RECOMMENDED ENHANCEMENT

Additional food stations could be set up in the reception area in such a manner as to draw guests into the room and encourage them to view the silent auction items. A selection of appropriate cheese and meats accompanied by gourmet crackers, lavosh and baguettes in addition to an assortment of seasonal grilled vegetables and fitting condiments would be served.

RECEPTION ICEBREAKERS—MIXING AND MINGLING SUGGESTIONS

Silent Auction

Culinary arts demonstration by a renowned wine country chef. Autographed cookbooks or demonstrated recipes can be purchased, with a portion of the proceeds donated to the charity.

Wine expert on hand to speak with guests about the wines being served during the reception period and those being auctioned later in the evening (some prized wines that are to be auctioned off could be on display). Wine expert could also discuss the wines being served over the course of dinner. As each course is being presented and the wine being poured, the expert can offer guests insight as to the pairing of the wine and the food.

Barrel Tasting

Top-of-the-barrel wine tasting.

Vertical Tasting

A vertical tasting would provide guests with an opportunity to sample different vintages (years), for example across a period of 10 years, of the same type of wine from the same district or vintner.

Horizontal Tasting

A horizontal tasting is based on the same vintage but different wine districts.

Different types of wines (e.g., ice wines, late harvest wines, or the best Chardonnays or Sauternes) could also be featured.

BACKGROUND RECEPTION MUSIC

Classical or jazz.

DECOR

Accent touches using grapevine, spring flowers, earth and moss would create an earthy vineyard feel.

DINNER MENU SUGGESTIONS

Dinner—Minimum five-course dinner recommended with suitable wines.

Dinner Menu Considerations:

Sample One—Plated

Appetizer—Seafood	Grilled Prawns
Appetizer—Meat	Foie Gras
Salad	Mixed Greens with Goat Cheese
Entree	Beef served with Horseradish, Mashed Potatoes and Asparagus
Dessert	Almond Raspberry Tart

Sample Two—Plated

Appetizer—Seafood	Lobster
Appetizer—Meat	Roasted Squab Breast
Salad	Mixed Greens with Foie Gras
Entree	Roasted Veal with Risotto and Seasoned Vegetables
Dessert	Orange Crème Brule with Raspberry

Optional—Intermezzo Course (served following the salad course)

Intermezzo	Chilled Sliced Melons or Seasonal Sorbets

Sample Three—Vintners' Gourmet Buffet

Include in your buffet selections salad and entree dishes based on:

Seafood	Lobster Salad with Cucumber Crabcakes with Gourmet Mustards Shrimp Salmon Tuna
Meat	Roasted Quail Roasted Beef Veal Lamb
Starches	Potato Risotto
Flavorings	Goat Cheese (in tartlets or salads) Caviar (on its own with condiments or on quail eggs, pancakes or blinis)
Vegetables	Mushrooms Truffles Artichokes Asparagus Fennel
Dessert	Strawberries or Raspberries White Chocolate Chocolate Truffles

When selecting your menu we would focus on featuring the bounty of your region and the harvesting of the fruits and vegetables of the season. Items offered at the reception would not be duplicated in the dinner menu.

THE WINE

We would work with the chef and wine expert to create menus that would complement the wines you have selected to fit in your budget requirements.

Wine service would be in large bottle format. Using magnums and three-liter bottles gives a more sensational presentation. Wait-staff would do a "parade of the big bottles" around the room before beginning the wine service.

PARADE OF THE BIG BOTTLES ENHANCEMENT

Heralding trumpeters can be used to draw attention to the procession.

Recommend using reserve wines (barrel selection of the finest lots from an exceptional vintage) or library wines (re-released wines that have aged in the winery's own stone cellars) with the meal.

EVENT RECOMMENDATION

For added appeal, have a celebrity chef custom-create and prepare your meal. A one-of-a-kind menu created especially for the event by a master chef could lend itself to becoming an annual fundraising endeavor.

PLACE CARDS

Auction paddles each with guest's name handlettered on the handle. One side of the auction paddle would be imprinted with the theme and logos of the sponsors. The auction paddle would also serve as the guest's take-home gift and be a memento of the evening.

CENTERPIECES

Instead of having a traditional floral display, consider a display that can become a part of the auction as a raffle or bid item, such as a basket made up of your wine country's specialty items donated by local vendors. Baskets could include cheeses, assorted biscuits and local delicacies such as mustard, oil, vinegar, preserves, gourmet chocolates and specialty wine items.

TABLE ASSIGNMENT

Tables can be named after specific types of wine, wine regions or wineries.

WINE AUCTION CATEGORIES

Live auction categories can include:

- Auction lots
- Private donor contributions
- Donated items from artists and cellar builders
- Lots plus crystal goblets and decanters
- Lots plus private dinners

SUGGESTED EVENT FLOW

Reception	Champagne and Caviar
	Classical Background Music
	Silent Auction
Dinner	Welcome by Chair/Emcee
	Heralding Trumpeters
	Parade of the Big Bottle
	Plated Dinner
	Big Bottle Wine Service
	Background Music
	Wine Auction
	Dancing, Music Performance or Review

SAMPLE C: CONCEPT FOR A THEME EVENT

THE EVENT

Society Gala Ball; One theme—"Moonlight and Magnolia"—with two design concepts.

THE THEME (1)

Moonlight and Magnolia—with a Southern Accent.

THE SETTING

The perfect setting for your Moonlight and Magnolia theme ball would be to take over a plantation house or private mansion exclusively for your event. Alternatively, the same feeling could be recreated in a ballroom. Here, you would want to create vignettes with wrought iron gates, moss-laden oak trees and fragrant magnolias lining paved walkways. The mood can be expanded by the use of gaslights, gazebos, fountains and even wooden porch swings. A backdrop of a southern plantation house would add to the setting. Guests would be requested to come in period dress of black tie or ball gown.

PARTY ELEMENTS

Invitation Options

An imprinted invitation on an 1860s replica dance card.

Old-fashioned fans inscribed with event details.

One lace fingerless glove boxed in black velvet with a formal invitation setting the mood of your event.

RECEPTION

In keeping with the theme, guests could be greeted by waitstaff in period dress serving mint juleps in frosted glasses on silver trays. Hard and soft lemonade could be served, as well as bloody Marys, iced tea or punch. The lemonade and the punch would be served from punchbowls.

Dry snacks in keeping with the southern theme could feature spiced pecans.

RECEPTION ICEBREAKERS—MIXING AND MINGLING SUGGESTIONS

Actual dance cards/programs could be handed out at registration and filled in by guests during cocktails.

Scarlett O'Hara and Rhett Butler look-a-likes handing out magnolia wristlets (real or artificial) to the ladies and boutonnieres to the men.

BACKGROUND RECEPTION MUSIC

Gospel/spiritual singers.

DECOR

Accent touches using mint green and gold damask in keeping with the colors of the period.

Empire and Federal period antiques.

DINNER MENU SUGGESTIONS

Dinner—Buffet or Plated

Seafood	Crawfish Fritters Pecan-Crusted Trout Large Jumbo Shrimp
Meat	Southern Fried Chicken (boneless/bite-sized) Sugar-Cured Hams Chicken and Dumplings Roast Turkey Stuffed with Cornbread BBQ Ribs (tender and cut, easy to manage)
Starches	Potato Salad Sweet Potato Cups or Pie Grits and Gravy Hopping John (rice and black-eyed peas) Biscuits (not hot rolls)
Vegetables	Savory Turnip Greens Asparagus Fried Green Tomatoes
Dessert	Strawberry Shortcake Old-Fashioned Bread Pudding Lemon Pie Pecan Pie with Ice Cream

Event Recommendation

To create a feeling of opulence and lavish entertainment, which is associated with southern hospitality, grace and charm, we recommend serving soup from soup tureens, displaying food on platters set out on antique side tables and oversized tables with pink floral china for a romantic feel, and using traditional silverware and cut crystal.

Suggested Event Flow

Reception	Passed Mint Juleps
	Gospel/Spiritual Background Music
Dinner	Buffet or Plated Dinner
	Wine Service
	Background Dinner Music
	Choreographed Dance Performance
	Guest Dance Instruction
	Dancing

The Theme (2)

Moonlight and Magnolia—Dancing in the Moonlight.

The Setting

The room would be piped and draped in fiber-optic curtains and with special effects created with the use of theatrical lighting. Your guests would experience the effect of stepping into a room completely filled with twinkling lights. Intelligent moving lights produce a dramatic entrance into the room.

Lighting washes would help to create different moods throughout the evening.

Guests would be requested to come dressed in black, white and silver.

PARTY ELEMENTS

Invitation Options

A custom kaleidoscope filled with a multiple miniature images of magnolias mixed with sparkling crystals in rich night-hued tones of black and silver with the recipient's name embedded in the vision. Each kaleidoscope would be one-of-a-kind and would set the tone of anticipation of a one-of-a-kind event. The invitation would adorn the kaleidoscope.

Innovative paper invitations featuring the moonlight and magnolias theme and incorporating all three theme colors.

RECEPTION

White-glove service. Passed champagne and canapés on silver platters.

Should you wish to consider an open bar, serving guests a signature beverage in keeping with the theme such as a "Moon Beam" (amaretto and white crème de cacao over ice) adds an extra theme tie-in.

RECEPTION ICEBREAKERS—MIXING AND MINGLING SUGGESTIONS

The moonlight theme lends itself to what is in the stars for your guests. Astrology readings can be incorporated into your reception. Several reading styles will be available for guests to choose from.

BACKGROUND RECEPTION MUSIC

White baby grand with pianist in white tails.

DECOR

The tables and chairs would be covered in crushed black velvet cloth. The bands on the chair covers (back only) would be encrusted with sparkling rhinestones and crystals.

Silver charger plates, fine white china, heavy cut crystal glassware edged in silver and gleaming silverware would add to the setting. Candles flickering in polished silver candlestick holders enhance the table setting. Pinspotting would add drama to each table. Magnolias would be the flower of choice this evening.

Dinner Menu Suggestions

Dinner—Plated

The menu suggestions, keeping with the rich, sensual mood created by the room decor and the table treatments, include:

Appetizer	Warm Lobster Salad
Salad	Caesar Salad
Entree	Steak Diane Grilled Asparagus Roasted Garlic Mashed Potatoes
Dessert	Crème Brûlée with Raspberry Sauce Truffles

Event Recommendation

As guests enter the room and find their seating, background dinner music would feature theme-appropriate music, such as "Dancing in the Moonlight" by King Harvest. After a fabulous dinner served with fine wines and liqueurs, cigars would follow in a separate room for those who wish to indulge. A high-energy band would play for your guests' enjoyment and for the grand finale—a dazzling starburst of indoor fireworks and dramatic laser display set to music to light up the room.

Suggested Event Flow

Reception	Passed Champagne and Canapés Pianist in White Tails Astrology Readings
Dinner	Plated Dinner Wine Service Background Music High-Energy Dance Band Grand Finale

INDEX

ABOUT THE AUTHOR

Judy **Allen** is one of the world's leading authorities on staging, event and lifestyle design and the bestselling author of ten books for the professional, business and consumer markets. Allen, a master of creative design, has flawlessly executed successful special events—corporate, social, and celebrity—for up to 2,000 guests at a time in more than 30 countries around the world. She has designed and produced memorable events such as Disney's worldwide theatrical opening-night gala for *Beauty and the Beast,* and the orchestration of Oscar-winning director Norman Jewison's 25th anniversary celebration for *Fiddler on the Roof.*

Allen is highly skilled in staging events that are strategically designed to be one-of-kind experiences, and is a master of transforming the energy of an event environment by engaging the senses with trademark primary design principles. She has worked closely with CEOs, CFOs, presidents and their executive staff around the globe to create, implement and oversee their corporate and social business events.

The many diverse events that Allen has designed and executed extend from complex one-day events to elaborate arrangements of theme productions taking place over the course of a week. These events ranged from very exclusive VIP events to multimillion-dollar, multimedia fantasy extravaganzas including seven new-car product launches and involved high-tech stage and show productions.

Her website is www.2.jproductions.com.